Federal Tax Reform

Studies of Government Finance

FIRST SERIES

Federal Tax Reform

The Impossible Dream?

GEORGE F. BREAK

and JOSEPH A. PECHMAN

Studies of Government Finance

THE BROOKINGS INSTITUTION

WASHINGTON, D.C.

THE BROOKINGS INSTITUTION is an independent organization devoted to nonpartisan research, education, and publication in economics, government, foreign policy, and the social sciences generally. Its principal purposes are to aid in the development of sound public policies and to promote public understanding of issues of national importance.

The Institution was founded on December 8, 1927, to merge the activities of the Institute for Government Research, founded in 1916, the Institute of Economics, founded in 1922, and the Robert Brookings Graduate School of Economics and Government, founded in 1924.

The Board of Trustees is responsible for the general administration of the Institution, while the immediate direction of the policies, program, and staff is vested in the President, assisted by an advisory committee of the officers and staff. The by-laws of the Institution state: "It is the function of the Trustees to make possible the conduct of scientific research, and publication, under the most favorable conditions, and to safeguard the independence of the research staff in the pursuit of their studies and in the publication of the results of such studies. It is not a part of their function to determine, control, or influence the conduct of particular investigations or the conclusions reached."

The President bears final responsibility for the decision to publish a manuscript as a Brookings book. In reaching his judgment on the competence, accuracy, and objectivity of each study, the President is advised by the director of the appropriate research program and weighs the views of a panel of expert outside readers who report to him in confidence on the quality of the work. Publication of a work signifies that it is deemed a competent treatment worthy of public consideration but does not imply endorsement of conclusions or recommendations.

The Institution maintains its position of neutrality on issues of public policy in order to safeguard the intellectual freedom of the staff. Hence interpretations or conclusions in Brookings publications should be understood to be solely those of the authors and should not be attributed to the Institution, to its trustees, officers, or other staff members, or to the organizations that support its research.

Foreword

THE FEDERAL tax structure has remained substantially unchanged since the enactment of the Tax Reform Act of 1969. Payroll taxes have been increased, income taxes have been reduced, and the investment tax credit has been suspended, reinstated, and then increased. But the basic structure of the income and payroll taxes, which now account for over 90 percent of federal tax revenue, has not been altered.

That the tax structure has been relatively stable does not mean that it enjoys general public approval. Many taxpayers, including both conservatives and liberals, regard it as unfair. The 1969 legislation, which was enacted in response to public pressure, was expected to be a first step in reforming the tax system, but no further steps have yet been taken. The House Ways and Means Committee held extensive hearings on tax reform in 1973 and, in the following year, completed a bill that was never seriously considered by the House or the Senate. Despite the legislative impasse, interest in tax reform has not abated. It was an issue in the 1972 and 1974 elections, and the congressional tax-writing committees have promised action at an early date.

Tax reform is urged not only for economic and equity reasons, but also because the tax system has become extremely complicated. Congress has repeatedly added new provisions to the tax laws in its effort to balance the competing demands of various groups. The result is an Internal Revenue Code well-nigh impenetrable to all but the expert.

Progress in reforming and simplifying the tax structure is slow because the subject matter is difficult for most people to understand and the issues are complex. The purpose of this book is to explain briefly, and in nontechnical terms, the major controversial elements of the tax system and of various tax reform proposals, so that interested persons will be able to make their own judgments. For more information on the issues and different points of view, readers are urged to refer to the bibliography at the end of the book.

The authors, George F. Break, professor of economics at the University of California (Berkeley) and a member of the associated staff of the Brookings Institution, and Joseph A. Pechman, director of the Brookings Economic Studies program, have had long experience in tax research and in the tax legislative process. They acknowledge with gratitude the work of Barry J. Eichengreen, who programmed most of the quantitative material in this volume on the computer, of Larry J. Tenison, who assisted in the programming, and of Catherine Armington, who acted as adviser on computer problems for the project. The authors are also grateful to Harvey E. Brazer, Charles E. McLure, Jr., Benjamin A. Okner, Stanford G. Ross, Emil H. Sunley, Jr., Stanley S. Surrey, and Bernard Wolfman for their comments and suggestions and to Gerald R. Jantscher, James R. Nunns, and Thomas E. Vasquez for their assistance in the preparation of the revenue estimates. Mary Bell Hevener, Clarence Otis, and Evelyn P. Fisher checked the manuscript for accuracy. Elizabeth H. Cross edited the volume and Florence Robinson prepared the index.

This is the second volume in the Brookings Studies of Government Finance, second series, which is devoted to examining issues in taxation and public expenditure policy. The preparation of this volume was supported by grants from the Carnegie Corporation of New York and the Richard K. Mellon Foundation for research at Brookings on federal budget policy. Research on the revenue implications of various tax proposals was supported by a grant from the RANN program of the National Science Foundation.

The authors' views are their own and should not be ascribed to the trustees, officers, or other staff members of the Brookings Institution, or to the Carnegie Corporation, the Richard K. Mellon Foundation, or the National Science Foundation.

KERMIT GORDON
President

June 1975
Washington, D.C.

Contents

Tables

Figure

CHAPTER ONE

Introduction

FEDERAL, state, and local government receipts now make up nearly one-third of the gross national product. Taxes, which constitute 95 percent of these receipts, include levies on a broad range of bases: corporate and individual incomes, general and selective sales, payrolls, property, and estates and gifts. The other 5 percent comes from nontax sources such as fees, user charges, and public enterprise profits.

Although the amount of tax money collected—$396 billion in 1973—may seem large, U.S. taxes are by no means the heaviest in the world. In 1972, for example, taxes were 28 percent of the gross national product in the United States but over 30 percent in eleven other developed countries (see table 1-1). These proportions ranged from 31 and 34 percent of GNP in Italy and Canada to 42 to 46 percent in Norway, Sweden, the Netherlands, and Denmark. Only Australia, Switzerland, and Japan have lower tax burdens than the United States.

Main Features of the U.S. Tax System

Compared to other developed countries, the United States makes relatively heavy use of income and property taxes and relatively light use of sales and social security levies. Of fifteen developed countries,

Table 1-1. Taxes as a Percent of Gross National Product and Distribution of Revenues by Major Tax Source, Selected Countries, 1972ᵃ

Country	Taxes as a percent of GNP	*Percentage distribution by major tax source*					
		Indi-vidual income	Corpora-tion income	Pay-rolls	Goods and servicesᵇ	Property	Death and gift
Norway	45.7	27	2	27	41	2	*
Denmark	44.8	48	2	8	38	4	*
Sweden	43.9	42	4	23	30	1	*
Netherlands	41.8	28	7	35	28	2	*
Austria	37.0	23	4	33	38	2	*
Germany	36.0	28	5	34	30	2	*
France	35.8	11	6	41	40	1	1
Belgium	35.2	27	7	30	34	...	1
United Kingdom	34.7	32	7	18	30	11	2
Canada	33.5	34	11	9	34	11	1
Italy	31.1	13	7	39	39	1	1
United States	28.1	34	11	20	19	13	2
Australia	24.3	38	16	4	34	6	2
Switzerland	24.1	33	8	23	28	6	1
Japan	21.1	26	24ᶜ	19	24ᶜ	5	2

Source: Organisation for Economic Co-operation and Development, *Revenue Statistics of OECD Member Countries, 1965–1972* (Paris: OECD, 1975). Data are on a calendar year basis for all countries except Denmark and Canada (year begins April 1) and the United States and Australia (year begins July 1). Figures are rounded.

* Less than 0.5 percent.

a. Includes national and local taxes.

b. Includes net revenues of utilities and liquor stores, receipts from licenses, fees and other charges, stamp taxes on transfers of property and securities, and other transactions taxes paid by enterprises.

c. The Japanese enterprise tax levied by prefectural governments is included in the corporation income tax and excluded from the tax on goods and services.

for example, the United States in 1972 raised a larger share of its tax revenues from property taxes than did any other country, and it and Canada ranked fifth in their relative use of income taxes. At the same time the United States ranked tenth in the proportion of its tax revenues obtained from payroll taxes and last in its reliance on sales and excise taxes.

Such international comparisons, while interesting, must be interpreted cautiously. It would be a mistake, for instance, to conclude from these figures that consumers, compared with income receivers and holders of wealth, really get off more lightly in the United States than they do elsewhere. The difficulty is that there is no accurate way of measuring the extent to which the property and corporation profits taxes, though nominally levied on property values and income, are actually shifted to consumers. That and other uncertainties about tax incidence make comparing the burdens of particular individuals or businesses conjectural. Nevertheless, it is clear that the *total* tax burden is more moderate in the United States than in most other developed countries.

One distinctive feature of the U.S. tax system is its federal structure. The national and state governments have sovereign taxing powers whereas local governments have such taxing powers as their state governments allow them. The federal government now raises 65 percent of all tax revenues and does so in ways that have remained broadly unchanged since World War II. This is not to say that the federal tax structure has been static. While its component parts have remained much the same, rate and structural adjustments have combined with major changes in the economy to produce important shifts in the roles of the various taxes. Income tax rates were lowered in 1964, and in 1969, 1971, and 1975 personal exemptions and deductions were liberalized so as to reduce tax burdens on low-income families, but payroll tax burdens on the same families have increased. The income tax rate reductions of the early 1960s were more than offset a decade later by inflation, which reduced the real value of both the personal exemption and the minimum standard deduction and pushed money incomes into higher and higher brackets. Effective tax rates were thus raised without statutory adjustments. Though the nominal corporate tax rate remained at 48 percent on profits in excess of $25,000, increasingly generous depreciation allowances, together with the investment tax credit and other special provisions, have operated to make actual burdens closer to 35 percent on the average, and much lower than that for specific industries. Finally, the federal excise tax system, which covered a wide variety of goods in the early postwar years, has been gradually whittled down until it is now limited mainly to sumptuary levies on liquor and tobacco, user taxes on road and air transportation, and a tax on telephone bills that is scheduled to be phased out at the end of 1981.

Still further changes in the federal tax system can be expected. Tax rates will be raised or lowered as domestic social priorities change and as international responsibilities and tension ebb and flow. Every time that happens, opportunities to improve the tax system will be presented to policymakers. Meanwhile the eternal cry for tax reform may gather enough political strength to force adjustments in the allocation of federal taxes. Regardless of which way tax reform is to be achieved, specific guidelines for action are needed. These can be useful only if they are developed from a full understanding of the basic goals and principles of taxation.

Goals and Principles of Taxation

The primary goal of taxation is to transfer control of resources from one group in the society to another and to do so in ways that do not jeopardize, and may even facilitate, the attainment of other economic goals. The transfers may be of two general kinds. The first shifts purchasing power from one group to another in the private sector of the economy; these are aimed at making the distribution of private income and wealth conform to the distribution that society views as desirable. The relevant instruments are taxes on those with too much income and wealth and transfer payments to those with too little. The second type shifts actual control of resources from the private to the public sector in pursuit of a wide and complex range of social priorities, such as transportation, health care, education, and housing. If such resource shifts, which determine the direct contribution of government to the gross national product, are to be accomplished without interfering with other economic goals, the operations must be financed by taxation or direct charges.

Taxation in modern societies is also, along with a broad set of other policy instruments, a means of achieving such standard economic goals as price stability, high employment, satisfactory growth, appropriate controls over the environmental effects of private activity, and suitable levels of international monetary reserves. Although in principle one can separate the stabilization and regulatory functions of taxation from the general revenue function of financing transfers and government purchases of goods and services, in practice most taxes either serve both purposes simultaneously or serve one purpose at the expense of the other. There is, in short, no simple distinction between the two separate functions of taxation.

In the pursuit of the goals of taxation, it is important that the tax system conform to certain well-established principles or canons. The first two principles—equity and economic efficiency—are fundamental means of achieving the main goals of taxation. The other principles are essential characteristics of any good tax, irrespective of its function or purpose. These are fiscal efficiency, simplicity, and certainty.

Equity

An equitable tax system treats in the same way all persons who are in the same economic situation—who, for example, have the same annual income—and makes suitable distinctions in its treatment of those who are in different economic circumstances. The first requirement, having to do with the like treatment of likes, is known as horizontal equity, and the second, having to do mainly with the distribution of tax burdens among people with different amounts of income and wealth, is known as vertical equity. Neither is a simple principle to apply.

The road to tax equity begins with the determination of an objective, unambiguous measure of each person's ability to pay taxes. Unfortunately, tax specialists do not agree on the ideal way to arrive at this measure. There is wide, though not universal, support for personal economic income, broadly defined as including all gains received by an individual during a given period of time. These gains must, to be complete, represent both what is consumed and what is saved.[1] Translating a comprehensive concept of economic income into a practicable tax base is no easy task, but advocates of this view hold that, unless all major gains are included, some persons' ability to pay will be more correctly measured than others', and equity will suffer. The other school of thought prefers to exclude saving from the measure of taxable income and to use as the tax base only what is spent on personal consumption during a given period of time.[2] Supporters of this position would in effect replace part or all of the income tax with a spendings tax. Interesting as such an alternative may be, the concept of economic income has traditionally prevailed in this country. This book will therefore adopt the majority position

1. For a discussion of this concept of income, known as the Haig-Simons concept, in the context of the federal income tax structure, see Joseph A. Pechman, *Federal Tax Policy*, revised edition (Brookings Institution, 1971), chapter 4. More technical analyses are available in Henry C. Simons, *Personal Income Taxation* (University of Chicago Press, 1938), and Richard Goode, *The Individual Income Tax*, revised edition (Brookings Institution, 1975).

2. See Nicholas Kaldor, *An Expenditure Tax* (London: George Allen and Unwin, 1955), and William D. Andrews, "A Consumption-Type or Cash Flow Personal Income Tax," *Harvard Law Review*, vol. 87 (April 1974), pp. 1113–88.

and accept economic income as its standard in evaluating proposed methods of improving the federal individual and corporation income taxes. Addition of a personal spendings, retail sales, or value-added tax to the federal revenue system may become an important policy issue in the future, but that would be matter for another book.

Establishment of the fundamental terms according to which tax-paying ability is to be measured is only the first step toward the achievement of equity, for the application of these terms immediately raises a host of questions. Clearly, horizontal equity does not mean that all families with the same income should be liable for the same amount of tax, for other criteria also affect ability to pay. The number of dependents a family must support or the burden it must carry in the form of extraordinary medical expenses or losses from natural catastrophe obviously has a direct effect on its taxpaying capability, as do many other variables. Hence equity requires adjusting the standard of income measurement to these differing capabilities while keeping the adjustment criteria as free of special provisions and ambiguities as possible.

While most people subscribe to at least the general principle of horizontal equity, vertical equity stirs perennial and unrelenting controversy. Few can view with dispassion questions concerning how much greater or smaller the tax burdens should be on people with more or less income than they themselves enjoy. For some any tax is a good tax as long as it is paid by someone else; others, only slightly more sophisticated, think that tax increases should only apply to persons wealthier than themselves. Some oppose low, or zero, tax burdens on families with incomes below official poverty levels, on the grounds that shouldering the responsibility of tax payments is an essential element in responsible citizen participation in governmental choices and decisions. Still others believe that the poor should be relieved of the burden of taxation to the extent practical.

Stated in more general terms, the basic issue is whether tax burdens should be the same percentage of income at all income levels (proportional taxation), or whether the percentage should rise as income rises (progressive taxation) or fall as income rises (regressive taxation). Though more honored in the breach than the observance, progressive taxation appears to be the choice of modern democratic societies. Making that choice, however, only begins to attack the problem. How progressive should tax burdens be? Should the degree of progression be uniform for all income ranges, or should it be higher for some and lower for others?[3] How high should the top tax rates be, and how low the bottom ones? Over what range of income, if any, should tax rates be zero? These are some of the difficult policy questions whose answers determine the vertical equity of any existing tax system.[4]

Economic Efficiency

The prime goal of any economy is to obtain from its limited supply of resources the highest possible output, defined broadly to include not only all the goods and services that make up the gross national product but also all the intangible values affecting the quality of life that are of increasing public concern. A good tax system is one that furthers that goal wherever it can and otherwise hinders it as little as possible. The problems here come not in the acceptance of the principle but in its implementation.

For some the best way to proceed is to seek a perfectly neutral set of general revenue taxes—that is, one that would raise money without causing anyone to change his economic behavior simply because of the way in which that money was taken from him. A neutral tax, in other words, would not lead anyone to work harder or to take more leisure, to save more or less, to invest in certain securities and not in others, or to buy one type of consumer goods rather than others. While neutral taxation appealed to the classical laissez-faire economists (because they believed that private markets functioned best when left entirely alone by governments), its appeal today is quite different. Few now believe in the inherent efficiency, or optimality, of private markets, and most support varying degrees and kinds of government regulation of those markets. What dis-

3. Since there is no single correct measure of the degree of progression, a given tax change may increase that degree according to one or two of the generally accepted measures but reduce it according to the third. These refinements, however, are not of concern in this book. For a comparison of the three alternative measures of the degree of progression, see Richard A. and Peggy B. Musgrave, *Public Finance in Theory and Practice* (McGraw-Hill, 1973), pp. 261–63. See also pp. 41–43 below.

4. Still another important question is whether and to what extent tax rates should be negative at the bottom of the income scale. Analysis of this issue, however, involves complex interactions with government welfare programs, income maintenance transfers, and various subsidies and lies outside the scope of this discussion. Here the only concern is the equity of the positive tax system.

tinguishes the proponents of neutral taxation today is their belief that such regulation is best done either by nontax fiscal instruments or by special kinds of regulatory fiscal devices not designed to raise revenue. If economic efficiency is achieved by these means, general revenue taxation is needed only to finance government purchases of goods and services or to alter the distribution of private income and wealth, and it should carry out those functions as neutrally as possible.

Critics of neutrality as a basic tax canon stress both the difficulties of achieving economic efficiency and the low probability that the government will accomplish much in this area. If it is to succeed at all, they argue, it must use every available instrument, including general revenue taxation. Neutral financing of government programs that allocate resources to be used for the greatest public good is not enough. A still better tax system, the argument continues, is one that in the process of raising general revenue helps to move private uses of resources toward the same social goals. It is clear that this optimizing criterion for taxation, as it may be called, is a good deal more complicated than the neutrality test. Judged on grounds of neutrality, any tax effect on private behavior would be a mark against the tax in question, but the optimization requirement necessitates making a careful distinction between good and bad effects, and they become important elements in the choice among alternative tax instruments.

Critics of this optimization approach stress both the difficulties of implementing it and the risks that it will be carried much too far. It may be only a small step, they argue, from searching actively for general revenue taxes that have desirable economic side effects to deliberately building into the tax structure incentives and reliefs to produce effects which could also be generated by government expenditure programs. Such provisions are highly controversial. To some they are the essence of a flexible and pluralistic approach to economic efficiency; to others they represent questionable subsidies, hidden from congressional and public scrutiny and serving mainly to enrich their beneficiaries.

Regardless of whether one tends to favor passive neutrality or active optimization as the proper role of a good tax system, the nature and size of its effects on the allocation of resources are important aspects of its performance. These must be determined in any case, and full display and discussion may do much to resolve their proper weight in the evaluation of tax reform proposals.

Fiscal Efficiency

A good tax is one that can be both administered by the government and complied with by the taxpayer at low cost. This means, for one thing, that enough money should be raised from a tax to permit realization of any possible economies of scale. It has been suggested, for example, that enactment of a federal sales or value-added tax would not be worthwhile unless it raised revenues of at least $10 billion a year. A second consideration is the nature of the trade-off between fiscal efficiency and equity. Up to some difficult-to-determine point higher administrative costs purchase equity-improvement benefits of equal or higher value to the society. Better administration and more carefully drafted tax laws can also limit the occurrence of various unintended, and frequently economically adverse, allocational effects of taxation. The best tax system, in short, is one with optimal rather than minimal administrative and compliance costs.

Simplicity

Another trade-off that must be coped with in tax policy is that between simplicity and the other characteristics of a good tax system. Simplicity does not mean that those whose economic affairs are inherently complex should expect to find determination of their tax burdens any less so. It does, however, imply that the distinctions made in the tax law for social and economic purposes should be kept to a minimum, so that tax information can be easily obtained from business accounting records and most ordinary taxpayers can prepare their income tax returns without professional advice and assistance. Simplicity also contributes to tax equity by enabling those with limited education to compute their correct tax bases as readily as those with more expertise and knowledge.[5]

5. The Swedish income tax has recently been criticized for lacking this kind of equity-enhancing simplicity. See Joachim Vogel, "Taxation and Public Opinion in Sweden: An Interpretation of Recent Survey Data," *National Tax Journal,* vol. 27 (December 1974), pp. 499–513.

Certainty

Modern governments have come a long way from the frustrating uncertainties that accompanied the old system of farming out tax-collecting rights to the highest bidder. Yet various problems remain. When the tax law is complex and imprecise, courts may interpret it variously, so that the tax consequences of certain activities may not be known in advance, or may differ from one part of the country to another pending a definitive ruling by a higher court. Some uncertainty of this sort may be eliminated by the issuance of advance Internal Revenue Service rulings, but others remain and affect business decisions in significant ways. Another uncertainty is illustrated by the omission of such important sources of income as housewives' services to the family or housing services to home owner-occupants, which are difficult to value properly for tax purposes. Leaving such significant imputed income untaxed creates interfamily tax inequities that can be only partially mitigated by the use of various second-best solutions; these, in turn, increase tax law complexity. Then there is the uncertainty about the market value of unique or seldom-traded assets, such as business plant and equipment, expensive homes, and works of art. Some escape is possible through the application of more or less arbitrary rules, such as those used in tax-depreciation accounting, but only at the cost of less tax equity. In other cases, such as pricing works of art donated to charities, the tax administration must rely on estimates prepared by experts.

Main Deficiencies of the Federal Tax System

While the U.S. tax system has many deficiencies, it is well to begin a discussion of them on a mild note of optimism. Compared to those of most other countries, the federal part of the U.S. tax system is probably one of the best. It relies heavily on progressive taxes and is administered with competence and evenhandedness. There is nonetheless ample room for improvement on the basis of any of the tests just discussed. Major horizontal inequities are created by special tax provisions at all income levels. The problem is to distinguish those that are justified by other considerations from those that are not. Average federal tax burdens are either proportional to

Table 1-2. **Effective Rates of Federal Taxes under the Most Progressive and Least Progressive Sets of Incidence Assumptions, by Population Decile, 1966**
Percent

Population decile[a]	Most progressive[b]	Least progressive[c]
First	7.8	13.8
Second	10.2	13.7
Third	13.5	15.8
Fourth	15.1	16.8
Fifth	15.9	17.4
Sixth	16.1	17.4
Seventh	16.2	17.5
Eighth	16.6	17.7
Ninth	16.7	17.6
Tenth	21.1	19.2
All deciles	17.6[d]	17.9[d]

Source: Joseph A. Pechman and Benjamin A. Okner, *Who Bears the Tax Burden?* (Brookings Institution, 1974), p. 64.

a. Population deciles are in order of comprehensive income, ranked from low to high.

b. Assumes that half the corporation income tax is borne by shareholders and half by owners of capital in general.

c. Assumes that one-quarter of the corporation income tax is borne by consumers, one-quarter by wage earners, and one-half by shareholders.

d. The average effective rates under the two sets of assumptions are slightly different because the amounts of income and taxes of the household sector depend on the incidence assumptions. See *Who Bears the Tax Burden?* pp. 39–42.

income or slightly progressive, depending on the assumptions made about the incidence of the corporation profits tax (see table 1-2). Imparting a more progressive slope to the tax system by one means or another is the major thrust of most reforming efforts.

A new front in the battle for tax reform was opened up in 1968 by Assistant Secretary of the Treasury for Tax Policy Stanley S. Surrey. Consolidating the somewhat scattered forces that had long been trying to expose and attack the wide variety of special provisions in the tax system for the purpose of achieving diverse social and economic goals, Surrey mounted a major campaign against what he called "tax expenditures." His analysis drew a line between income tax rules that are required to establish a comprehensive, equitable, efficient, and simple tax system and those set up deliberately to encourage certain private activities for sanctioned purposes by offering reductions in tax liabilities. Such subsidies, he argued, when proper at all, could in nearly every instance be better provided by direct government expenditure programs, since they would then be regularly reviewed by Congress and judged on the same basis as other government-financed activities. Paying for them instead by "tax expenditures," he contended, has the effect of obscuring their cost in inefficiency and inequity and keeping them sheltered from public view.[6]

A thorough review and evaluation of current tax expenditures would entail a threefold process: (1) determining whether the tax provision still serves a valid public purpose; (2) determining whether the public benefits generated by the provision exceed its costs; and (3) comparing the provision with alternative means of achieving the same public ends and deciding whether it is the best choice among these. Only tax expenditures that survived all three tests should be retained as part of the tax system. The significance of this reform proposal is shown by the Office of Management and Budget's official estimates of the size of the tax expenditures currently authorized— $92 billion for fiscal 1976, or roughly 26 percent of projected expenditures for that year (see table 1-3).[7] Few experts who have grappled with this question have any illusions about the difficulty of bringing about major changes, even in the name of reform. If agreement could be reached on the basic principle (and that is far from likely), there would still be widely differing opinions about which tax rules were legitimate requirements of a good tax system, which were tax expenditures, and how the relevant benefit-cost analyses should be interpreted.

A fundamental consideration that should be kept in mind in pursuing tax reform is that it might eliminate some tax distortions only to create others. The tightly defined, comprehensive income tax that is the essence of any reformer's goal would in itself produce unforeseen changes in private economic behavior. Of particular concern are possible disincentives to work or to save and invest. For this

6. See Stanley S. Surrey, *Pathways to Tax Reform* (Harvard University Press, 1973). For an earlier discussion of the same issues, see Bernard Wolfman, "Federal Tax Policy and the Support of Science," *University of Pennsylvania Law Review,* vol. 114 (December 1965), pp. 171–86.

7. *Special Analyses, Budget of the United States Government, Fiscal Year 1976,* table F-1, pp. 108–09. This does not include the revenue loss resulting from income splitting, the omission from the tax base of capital gains on assets transferred by gift or at death, the deferral of tax on foreign corporate income, the asset depreciation range system, and the maximum tax rate on earned income (see chapters 2 and 3 below).

reason, many reformers are careful to couple their proposals for a comprehensive tax system with a substantial reduction in tax rates.[8] Reform proposals that do not come to grips with the incentive questions do not deserve to be taken seriously.

The inevitable effect of this problem is to lend credence to the argument for tax diversification. The great weight the U.S. tax system puts on income taxation is a source of major concern to tax diversifiers. They stress the advantages of providing the government with a multiplicity of tax instruments as a means of escaping the limitations on both economic efficiency and interpersonal equity that excessive reliance on any single tax approach is apt to produce. Of equal importance is the necessity for providing the federal government with an adequate range of tax instruments to deal with the extremely complex economic functions it must carry out. Energy conservation policies calling for higher federal taxes on crude oil or gasoline, for example, may be stymied by a lack of some practical way to mitigate the adverse effects of the energy tax on low-income groups. Demand management tax policies must now rely mainly on income tax surcharges or rebates, though most economists would rate as more effective changes in the rates of a federal retail sales, value-added, or personal consumption tax. Whether variety is the spice needed to put greater life into the federal tax system, however, is a question of long-range tax policy and must run the exhaustive policy formulation gamut before its desirability can be demonstrated.

Practical Difficulties of Tax Reform

Why, it is often asked, if tax reform is so desirable, haven't we had more of it? One answer may be that the beauty of tax reform shines more brightly in the eyes of the reformers than in those of the general public. Another is that any kind of reform has a built-in dilemma. An approach that concentrates on a limited number of specific proposals immediately runs afoul of those who stand to lose by the change. Their cries are inevitably loud enough to drown out the praises of the few who are farsighted enough to perceive the

8. See Joseph A. Pechman and Benjamin A. Okner, "Individual Income Tax Erosion by Income Classes," *The Economics of Federal Subsidy Programs,* a compendium of papers submitted to the Joint Economic Committee, pt. 1, *General Study Papers,* 92 Cong. 2 sess. (1972), pp. 13–40 (Brookings Reprint 230).

**Table 1-3. Tax Expenditures of Individuals and Corporations,
by Budget Category, Fiscal Year 1976**

Millions of dollars

	Amount of tax expenditure		
Budget category and tax expenditure provision	*Individuals*	*Corporations*	*Total*
National defense			
Exclusion of benefits and allowances to armed forces personnel	650	...	650
Exclusion of military disability pensions	85	...	85
International affairs			
Exclusion of gross-up on dividends of corporations in less developed countries	...	55	55
Exclusion of income earned abroad by U.S. citizens	100	...	100
Deferral of income of domestic international sales corporations	...	1,320	1,320
Special rate for Western Hemisphere trade corporations	...	50	50
Agriculture			
Expensing of capital outlays	495	155	650
Capital gain treatment of certain income	340	25	365
Natural resources, environment, and energy			
Expensing of exploration and development costs	130	1,235	1,365
Excess of percentage over cost depletion	445	2,610	3,055
Capital gain treatment of royalties on coal and iron ore	...	5	5
Capital gain treatment of income from timber	60	155	215
Pollution control, 5-year amortization	...	20	20
Commerce and transportation			
$25,000 corporate surtax exemption	...	3,570	3,570
Deferral of tax on shipping companies	...	40	40
Railroad rolling stock, 5-year amortization	...	55	55
Bad debt reserve of financial institutions in excess of actual	...	980	980
Deductibility of nonbusiness state gasoline taxes	850	...	850
Community and regional development			
Housing rehabilitation, 5-year amortization	60	35	95
Education, manpower, and social services			
Child care facilities, 5-year amortization	...	5	5
Exclusion of scholarships and fellowships	190	...	190
Parental personal exemptions for students aged 19 and over	690	...	690
Deductibility of contributions to educational institutions	435	155	590
Deductibility of child and dependent care expenses	250	...	250
Credit for employing public assistance recipients under work incentive program	...	5	5
Health			
Exclusion of employer contributions to medical insurance premiums and medical care	3,745	...	3,745
Deductibility of medical expenses	2,630	...	2,630
Income security			
Exclusion of social security benefits			
Disability insurance benefits	280	...	280
OASI benefits for aged	2,940	...	2,940
Benefits for dependents and survivors	480	...	480
Exclusion of railroad retirement benefits	180	...	180
Exclusion of sick pay	295	...	295
Exclusion of unemployment insurance benefits	3,830	...	3,830
Exclusion of workmen's compensation benefits	620	...	620
Exclusion of public assistance benefits	90	...	90
Net exclusion of pension contributions and earnings			
Employer plans	5,740	...	5,740
Plans for self-employed and others	710	...	710
Exclusion of other employee benefits			
Premiums on group term life insurance	805	...	805
Premiums on accident and accidental death insurance	50	...	50
Privately financed supplementary unemployment benefits	5	...	5
Meals and lodging	190	...	190
Exclusion of capital gain on house sale if 65 or over	10	...	10
Excess of percentage standard deduction over minimum standard deduction	1,420	...	1,420

Table 1-3 (*continued*)

Budget category and tax expenditure provision	Amount of tax expenditure		
	Individuals	*Corporations*	*Total*
Additional exemption for the blind	15	...	15
Additional exemption for 65 and over	1,250	...	1,250
Retirement income credit	70	...	70
Veterans' benefits and services			
Exclusion of veterans' disability compensation	550	...	550
Exclusion of veterans' pensions	35	...	35
Exclusion of GI Bill benefits	250	...	250
General government			
Credits and deductions for political contributions	50	...	50
Revenue sharing and general purpose fiscal assistance			
Exclusion of interest on state and local debt	1,260	3,505	4,765
Exclusion of income earned in U.S. possessions	5	350	355
Deductibility of nonbusiness state and local taxes (other than on owner-occupied homes and gasoline)	9,950	...	9,950
Business investment			
Depreciation on rental housing in excess of straight-line	420	120	540
Depreciation on buildings (other than rental housing) in excess of straight-line	215	275	490
Expensing of research and development expenditures	...	660	660
Capital gain, corporate (other than farming and timber)	...	755	755
Investment credit	950	4,420	5,370
Personal investment			
Dividend exclusion	360	...	360
Capital gain, individual (other than farming and timber)	4,165	...	4,165
Exclusion of interest on life insurance savings	1,820	...	1,820
Deferral of capital gain on home sales	315	...	315
Deductibility of mortgage interest on owner-occupied homes	6,500	...	6,500
Deductibility of property taxes on owner-occupied homes	5,270	...	5,270
Deductibility of casualty losses	300	...	300
Other tax expenditures			
Exemption of credit unions	...	125	125
Deductibility of charitable contributions (other than education)	4,840	285	5,125
Deductibility of interest on consumer credit	3,460	...	3,460
Total, all tax expenditures[a]	70,850	20,970	91,820

Source: *Special Analyses, Budget of the United States Government, Fiscal Year 1976*, pp. 108–09. Estimates are based on the tax laws in effect on January 1, 1975.

a. The totals are the mathematical sums of the columns. Individual estimates in this table are based on the assumption that no other changes would be made in the tax law. Consequently, the aggregate revenue effect will not equal the sum of the revenue effects of the individual items shown.

potential gains for the general public. On the other hand, a reform program directed to grand and sweepingly comprehensive changes that would mean significant monetary gains for some and significant monetary losses for others is bound to arouse more hostility than support as the majority of people, unsure of their own prospects in the shifting scene, would rather bear the burdens they now have than accept the uncertain burdens of an alternative system.

Circumventing this dilemma is a task worthy of a Solomon. Somehow the balance must be redressed, particularly in congressional deliberations, between the vigilant and vocal special interests and the often-confused, usually inarticulate general taxpayer. What changes, if any, will be made in the U.S. tax system will depend largely on the persuasiveness of those presenting the case for tax reform. For if it does not serve the general welfare, tax reform is a costly kind of zero-sum game. It is zero-sum because pure tax reform, by definition, generates monetary gains to some taxpayers by imposing monetary losses of equal size on others. It is costly because no tax reform plan can be developed without much time and effort; moreover, discussion of who should gain and who should lose often creates divisive ill-will that any society would be better off without. If tax reform is no more than a blatant power struggle of conflicting special interests, in other words, it will not rate high on the agenda of urgent public policy issues. That tax reform will produce larger gains than losses and is therefore a positive-sum game well worth playing is the firm belief of most fiscal economists. Past failures in the tax reform movement may well be due mainly to the experts' lack of success in conveying this message to the general public.

The key to action on tax reform, then, is both a broader public agreement on the proper distributional, or equity, goals of society and a deeper public understanding of the contributions that a better tax system can make to the achievement of the best and most efficient use of the society's available resources. Bad taxes may counteract many of the intended good effects of government economic policies. Good taxes, in contrast, provide the lubrication essential to the smooth pursuance of the society's economic priorities.

Constructed as it must be from a complex set of trade-offs whose dimensions are uncertain and whose ingredients inspire sharply differing individual evaluations, a good tax system is a delicate, ever-changing work of political and economic artisanship. At one and the same time it must be:

—simple enough to be widely understood but complex enough to deal effectively with economic reality;

—equitable in its allocation of burdens between rich and poor but sensitive to the potential disincentive effects of high tax rates;

—frugal in its commitment of resources to administration and compliance but generous in applying them to the pursuit of fairness and justice;

—evenhanded in its treatment of similarly situated taxpayers but alert to the social benefits attainable with well-designed tax incentives.

It is little wonder that the exact dimensions of a better federal tax system are difficult to discern. Yet there do seem to be at least a few general qualities that would command wide agreement. One has to do with federal tax burdens on the lowest-income groups. That these burdens are excessive is a criticism by no means confined to the lowest-income groups themselves. Part of the problem is created by the heavy pressure exerted by the payroll tax for social security, and part stems from the effects of inflation on federal individual income tax liabilities. If all prices double (and since 1967 we have come more than halfway toward that point), a $4,000 poverty-line income is converted to an $8,000 one. Unless the personal exemptions are adjusted to allow for such monetary changes, the 1969 congressional decision (confirmed in 1971 and again in 1975) to exempt the poor from the federal individual income tax will be seriously eroded.

A second, and conspicuous, need is for greater uniformity of tax burdens, and hence greater horizontal equity, among families of similar circumstances in the middle and upper income ranges. This will entail a careful exploration of ways to integrate the corporation and personal income taxes as well as a thorough scrutiny of all tax expenditures to eliminate those that accomplish no significant social purpose or whose function could be more efficiently carried out by other fiscal instruments. Considerable skill and care will be needed in performing this surgery, since to some extent these provisions may have been useful as a safety valve for dissipating the excessive pressure of high tax rates on incentives to work and to save and invest. Since the available empirical evidence concerning tax disincentives is not definitive, it is difficult to determine whether reductions in the highest marginal tax rates should be an important goal of federal tax reform. In any case, broadening the federal income tax base, which is a major objective, will provide the opportunity for enactment of tax rate reductions that serve the causes of both equity and economic efficiency.

A third, though more controversial, reform objective is the diversification of federal revenue sources. One goal might be to shift some weight from the income tax to federal taxes on wealth and consumption. This could be done by strengthening and restructuring gift and estate taxes, by instituting progressive taxes on net wealth or personal consumption, or by enacting a national retail sales or value-added tax. Such diversification could also lighten the growing burden on the payroll tax, which has been the sole source of support for social insurance programs. But none of these potential new sources of federal revenue are dealt with in this book. Reform of the existing federal tax system seems a much more important matter for congressional attention for the next few years. Depending on what is done in that area and on many other economic developments, the adoption of some major new sources of federal tax revenue may— or may not—be a major policy issue in the years ahead.

The limited general agreement on any of the fundamental criteria for federal tax reform is evidence of the need for wider discussion and more sophisticated awareness of the issues. And the discussion must not be confined to broad policies, for the essence of a tax system is in the myriad complex details that really determine its impact. It is to these bread-and-butter issues that this volume is addressed.

Organization of the Book

The federal government derives its tax revenues from five major sources: the individual income tax, the corporation income tax, the payroll tax, the estate and gift taxes, and the excise taxes. Together, the two income taxes account for almost 60 percent of total tax revenues and the payroll taxes for over 30 percent; estate and gift taxes and excises are relatively minor sources (table 1-4). Although there is little disposition to drop any of the present sources, there is considerable criticism of the way in which each of the present taxes is levied. The next four chapters explain the structure of the various taxes and the reasons they are being criticized, and then discuss the major proposals that have been advanced to modify them.

The two income taxes—individual and corporation—are considered first because they complement one another. The individual income tax is regarded as the basic tax because only individuals have "ability to pay." However, a tax on individual income cannot be levied without at the same time doing something about corporation income, because individuals could avoid tax through corporate retentions. Moreover, many of the provisions applying to business and property income are the same for individuals and corporations. Chapter 2 is concerned with the structure of the income tax as it applies to individuals and households without regard to source of income. In chapter 3, the treatment of business and investment in-

Table 1-4. Estimated Distribution of Federal Tax Revenues, by Major Source,[a]
Fiscal Year 1975

Revenue source	Amount (billions of dollars)	Percentage distribution
Individual income tax	117.7	44.8
Corporation income tax	38.5	14.7
Payroll taxes	81.8	31.1
Estate and gift taxes	4.8	1.8
Excise taxes	19.9	7.6
Total	262.8	100.0

Source: *The Budget of the United States Government, Fiscal Year 1976*, p. 322. Figures are rounded.
a. Excludes customs duties, payments for supplementary medical insurance, employee contributions to federal retirement programs, nontax fees and charges, and other miscellaneous receipts.

come under both the individual and corporation income taxes is discussed. Chapter 4 deals with the relation between the two taxes.

The three tax sources other than the income taxes are analyzed in chapter 5. In recent years, concern has been expressed about the heavy burden of the payroll tax on the poor, and proposals have been made to alleviate this burden without impairing the financial solvency of the social security system. Such reform obviously depends on attitudes toward the financing of the social security system. No major changes have been made in estate and gift taxes since 1948, but most experts agree that they are greatly in need of reform. The problems here are not only technical but have social implications, and any effective reform would mean making substantial changes in the structure of these taxes. The selective excise taxes are now a minor source of revenue, but periodically it is suggested that some form of general consumption tax be added to the tax system. The major objection to such a tax is its regressivity.

Chapter 6 brings together the various tax reforms discussed in earlier chapters in several packages that would improve the horizontal equity of the tax system and moderately increase the progressivity of tax burdens. These tax packages would include rate reductions as well as structural adjustments in the major taxes. The feasibility of such changes in the tax system depends on the value placed by the public and Congress on reducing the great disparities in the tax burdens of people with the same income and the willingness of Congress to withstand the pressure of the traditional lobbies that benefit from the existing special provisions.

Finally, one feature of the revenue simulations presented through-out the book should be stressed. Since they were derived from the Brookings tax data file, there is no way to take into account taxpayer reaction to any of the proposed changes, although in reality such reaction could produce significant feedback effects on federal tax revenues. Eliminating the deductibility of state and local property taxes on owner-occupied homes, for example, might well induce those governments to gradually shift their tax systems to greater use of (deductible) sales and income taxes, and hence to reduce or even cancel out the federal revenue gains from the policy change. Poten-tial reactions of this kind may be important and must always be kept in mind. However, to attempt to identify them all and to quantify their effects would exceed not only the scope of this book but pos-sibly the present capabilities of economic science.

CHAPTER TWO

The Individual Income Tax

THE INDIVIDUAL income taxpayer calculates his tax liability in four steps. First, all taxable income receipts, after allowance for business expenses, are added to obtain *adjusted gross income.* Second, deductions are allowed for certain personal outlays (such as taxes, medical expenses, contributions) or, as an alternative, the taxpayer can elect a standard deduction. Third, the personal exemptions for himself and his family are subtracted. The amount left after subtracting the deductions and exemptions is the portion of his income that is actually subject to the tax rates, the *taxable income.* (The derivation of taxable income for all taxpayers in 1972 is given in table 2-1.) Finally, tax liability is figured from one of several rate schedules according to the taxpayer's marital status. Each step in these calculations raises difficult policy issues. The problems of defining adjusted gross income are discussed in the next chapter; the remaining steps in the tax calculation are discussed in this chapter.

Personal Deductions

The major function of personal deductions is to adjust for unusual circumstances that have a bearing on an individual's capacity to pay income taxes. One example of such a deduction is that for medical expenses. Clearly, a family with heavy medical payments is less able

Table 2-1. Derivation of Taxable Individual Income, 1972

Billions of dollars

Item	Amount
Total adjusted gross income (AGI)	798.4
Deduct: AGI not reported on tax returns	51.8
AGI reported on nontaxable returns	28.9
Equals: AGI on taxable returns	717.7
Deduct: Personal deductions on taxable returns	142.8
Equals: Net income before exemptions on taxable returns	574.9
Deduct: Personal exemptions on taxable returns	128.3
Equals: Taxable income of individuals	446.6

Source: *Survey of Current Business* (February 1975), p. 34.

to pay than a family with the same income and no medical expenses. Unfortunately, most of the deductions cannot be justified as a necessary refinement of taxable income; several are merely subsidies for particular types of expenditures that may not merit government encouragement. Such provisions reduce the tax base by billions of dollars without adding much to the equity of the income tax.

The major deductions are for state and local income, sales, property, and gasoline taxes, interest payments, medical and dental expenses, and charitable contributions.[1] In lieu of itemizing deductions, the taxpayer may elect to use a *standard deduction* of 16 percent of income, up to a maximum of $2,300 for single persons and $2,600 for married couples, or a *low-income allowance* of $1,600 for single persons and $1,900 for married couples. In 1972 personal deductions on taxable returns amounted to $143 billion (table 2-2), or 20 percent of adjusted gross income reported on these returns.

Deductions for state and local income taxes protect the taxpayer against tax rates that are excessively high when combined with the federal rate.[2] Deductions for sales and income taxes can also be justified as a method of encouraging the state and local governments to use these sources to raise needed revenues and of narrowing inter-

1. In addition, deductions are allowed for child care expenses, casualty losses in excess of $100 for each casualty, alimony payments, work-related expenses (such as outlays for necessary work clothes and union dues), and expenses of earning investment income.

2. Under some circumstances the top combined marginal rates could become confiscatory without this deduction. This was the case when the top federal rate was 90 percent or more, but it has not been true since 1965, when the present maximum rate of 70 percent became effective.

Table 2-2. Deductions Reported on Federal Individual Income Tax Returns, 1972
Billions of dollars

Deduction	Amount
Itemized	**92.0**
State and local taxes	35.1
Interest payments	26.1
Medical and dental expenses	8.7
Charitable contributions	12.8
Other[a]	9.2
Standard	**50.8**
Percentage deduction	23.9
Low-income allowance	26.9
Total	**142.8**

Source: U.S. Department of the Treasury, *Statistics of Income—1972, Individual Income Tax Returns* (1974), tables 1.4 and 2.4, pp. 20 and 92. Figures are rounded.

a. Includes deductions for child care, casualty losses, alimony payments, work-related expenses, expenses of earning investment income, and deductions not specified on tax returns.

state tax differences.[3] But this rationale does not apply to gasoline taxes, which are levied to pay for benefits received by highway users.

The deduction for the property tax paid by homeowners, which is used by every local government in the United States, is controversial.[4] Some argue that the deduction for residential property taxes is not appropriate because the tax receipts are used to pay for local services to property owners; others defend the deduction on the ground that the property tax is not purely a benefit tax and its use should be encouraged by the federal government as much as are state and local income and sales taxes.

Most of the interest deductions on federal tax returns are payments on consumer loans and home mortgages. The deduction for interest on consumer loans is clearly a subsidy to those who borrow for current consumption. The deductions for mortgage interest payments and the residential property tax would be appropriate if taxpayers were required to include the rental value of their homes in taxable income.[5] Under present circumstances the homeowner has a multiple tax ad-

3. For instance, if one state levies a 10 percent tax and another a 5 percent tax, the net cost (after allowing for the federal deduction) of the additional 5 percent tax for a taxpayer subject to a 70 percent federal marginal rate is only 1.5 percent.

4. The controversy does not extend to the deduction for property taxes paid by business firms. These payments are costs of doing business; to arrive at the net income of a business operation requires that they be deductible.

5. That the rental value of an owner-occupied home is "economic" income can be illustrated by the case of two persons, each occupying a $20,000 house that rents

vantage over the renter—he can omit the net rental value of his home from the tax base and can also deduct his mortgage interest and property tax payments. At 1976 income levels the total tax advantage will exceed $12 billion a year. Although many economists believe that the net rental value of owned homes should be taxable, most acknowledge that such a proposal would have little support from the public or in Congress. The property tax advantage can be eliminated, however, by eliminating the property tax deduction for homeowners. The interest advantage of consumers as well as of homeowners can be removed—without taxing the rental value of owner-occupied homes —by allowing a deduction for interest only to the extent of investment income an individual reports on his tax return. This would continue deductions for interest payments that are true business and investment costs and increase revenues by over $5 billion a year.

The medical expense deduction, which was enacted in 1942, when wartime requirements brought the personal exemption to a historic low, identifies unusual expenses as those that exceed a modest percentage of income. The "floor" was originally 5 percent but it was reduced to 3 percent in 1954. Recent data suggest that median outlays for medical and dental expenses are in excess of 3 percent of income,[6] so the 3 percent floor does not screen out much of the "usual" medical expense. A 5 percent floor would still permit 30 percent of families to deduct medical expenses and would thus be consistent with the basic rationale of the deduction.

In 1967 the medical expense deduction was expanded: one-half of the premiums paid for private health insurance, up to a maximum of $150, is deductible separately, without regard to the floor on other medical deductions; the remainder is deductible as a regular medical expense. This action was taken to encourage broadened coverage of private health insurance, but it is clearly not a substitute for national health insurance. The special deduction is hard to defend even now,

---

for $2,000 a year. The first rents the house and invests, say, $20,000 in securities yielding 10 percent. The $2,000 of interest or dividends he receives is taxable, but he is not allowed to deduct his rental payment. The second buys the same house for $20,000. He has no cash income from property yet receives the same $2,000 in housing services as the renter.

6. The median percentage of income spent on medical care was 3.4 percent in 1970, according to data from the 1970 Health Care Survey of the Center for Health Administration Studies, University of Chicago. We are indebted to Charles E. Phelps of the Rand Corporation for this information.

and it will certainly be unnecessary if a national health insurance plan is enacted.

Encouragement of charitable contributions through the tax system seems to have widespread support, but there is some debate about the form of the income tax deduction for such contributions. Some argue that the deduction should be replaced by a flat tax credit (say, 25 or 30 percent of the contribution) to equalize the subsidy rate among income classes.[7] Others believe that the deduction has little effect on the charitable giving of most taxpayers. They propose that the deduction be subject to a floor of 2 or 3 percent of income, thus saving revenue without discouraging larger-than-average giving.[8] However, Congress is hesitant to alter the form of the charitable deduction because a change might upset the traditional sources and volume of support of the recipient organizations.[9]

Finally, the standard deduction, which was intended to relieve taxpayers of the burden of itemizing their deductions, could be reduced if the itemized deductions were pruned. The standard deduction is currently applicable to the relatively narrow income ranges of $11,875 to $16,250 for married couples and $10,000 to $14,375 for single persons.[10] How much the standard deduction could be cut and still maintain its simplification objective would depend on the extent of the revisions in the itemized deductions. With sufficient pruning of itemized deductions, it would be possible to eliminate the percentage

7. A credit slightly smaller than 25 percent, if offered to all taxpayers, and one slightly larger than 25 percent, if restricted to taxpayers who itemize their deductions, would cost about the same amount of revenue as the present deduction. These estimates, which were recently prepared for the Commission on Private Philanthropy and Public Needs by Martin S. Feldstein and his associates, allow for the reactions of taxpayers to the change in the terms on which they could make contributions and for the feedback effects of these reactions on Treasury revenues.

8. The intent of the floor on charitable contributions could be subverted by bunching contributions for several years in one year. To prevent this from happening on a large scale, it might be necessary to average contributions and income over, say, a three-year period and permit a deduction for the excess of the average contribution over 2 or 3 percent of the average income. The same problem arises for the medical expense deduction, but it has not been considered serious enough to warrant the extra complications of averaging payments over a period of years.

9. The effect of changes in the tax incentive for charitable giving would depend on the income classes affected. High income taxpayers make most of their contributions to educational and research institutions, hospitals, and foundations; low income taxpayers give mainly to religious organizations.

10. The low-income allowance is more advantageous to the taxpayer below the lower limits; at the upper limits the maximum standard deductions apply.

Table 2-3. Increases in Revenue under Various Sets of Revisions of Personal Deductions under the Federal Individual Income Tax, 1976

Billions of dollars

Revision	Set A	Set B	Set C
Eliminate deduction for state gasoline taxes	0.8	0.8	0.8
Eliminate separate deduction for health insurance premiums	0.3	0.3	0.3
Raise floor on medical expense deduction from 3 to 5 percent	...	0.8	0.8
Introduce 2 percent floor in the charitable contribution deduction	...	2.5	2.5
Eliminate deduction for property taxes	...	...	4.6
Limit interest deduction to the amount of business and property income	...	...	5.2
Convert standard deduction and low-income allowance to a flat $2,000[a]	...	*	1.1
Total	1.1	4.4[b]	13.2[b]

Source: Brookings 1972 tax file, projected to 1976.
* Less than $50 million.
a. Assumes revisions in itemized deductions as indicated above.
b. Total is less than the sum of the individual revisions because the standard deduction would exceed the sum of the remaining deductions for many of those now itemizing deductions.

standard deduction and rely exclusively on the low-income allowance as an alternative to the itemized deductions.

Since the personal deductions amount to about a fifth of the taxable income reported on taxable returns, revision of the personal deductions could produce a substantial amount of revenue. The implications of three combinations of reforms are given in table 2-3. The gains in revenue, which vary from as little as $1 billion a year (at income levels projected for 1976) to as much as $13 billion a year, would result from increasing the tax burden of middle and upper income taxpayers relatively more than that for the lower income classes. If desired, however, offsetting tax reductions could be devised (such as larger exemptions and rate reductions) to avoid such increases in average tax burdens.

Thus far, the allowances for special personal outlays have been provided in the form of deductions from adjusted gross income in arriving at taxable income. This form of allowance is regarded by some as an "upside-down" subsidy, on the ground that the higher the income of the taxpayer, the larger the amount of tax reduction per dollar of outlay. Those who support this view argue that it would be more equitable to convert the deduction to a tax credit, so that taxpayers at all income levels would receive the same tax reduction per dollar of outlay. The same argument is made for converting the personal exemptions to a tax credit (see the next section). The rising value of a deduction is inherent in an income tax with graduated rates. The vertical distributional effects of a deduction can be approximately offset by changing the tax rates, so there is little point in converting the deduction to a credit. If it is not an appropriate refinement of income in judging relative tax liabilities, the deduction ought to be eliminated. If it were nevertheless decided to substitute, say, a 25 percent tax credit for all the deductions (standard as well as itemized) allowed under present law, revenues would be increased by about $6 billion a year.

Personal Exemptions

The major functions of the personal exemption are to remove from the tax rolls people who cannot pay and to differentiate among the tax liabilities of families of different size having the same income. Under present law, the same exemption is provided for each member of the family, and additional exemptions of the same amount are allowed for persons sixty-five and over and for those who are blind.

Since 1964 the minimum standard deduction—called the low-income allowance since 1971—has been used in conjunction with the personal exemption to raise the minimum taxable levels approximately to the estimated "poverty" levels. This device was adopted because the amount of money necessary to achieve a certain level of living does not rise in proportion to the number of persons in the family, so that the per capita exemption alone is not adequate for single persons and small families.[11]

During periods of inflation, unless adjustments are made periodically, the exemption and minimum standard deduction become increasingly inadequate. The last adjustment to the exemption was made effective for the income year 1972, when the present $750 per capita exemption was adopted. In 1975, the low-income allowance was increased from a flat $1,300 to $1,900 for married couples and $1,600 for single persons, and a $30 per capita credit was provided in lieu of an increase in the personal exemption. As a result the min-

11. The poverty levels are estimated annually from income surveys in U.S. Bureau of the Census, *Current Population Reports,* Series P-60, "Consumer Income."

Table 2-4. Minimum Taxable Levels under the 1974 and 1975 Individual Income Tax Laws Compared with Estimated Poverty Lines for 1975
Dollars

Number in family	1975 poverty line[a]	1974 law[b]		1975 law[c]	
		Minimum taxable level	Difference	Minimum taxable level	Difference
1	2,850	2,050	−800	2,564	−286
2	3,470	2,800	−670	3,829	359
3	4,253	3,550	−703	4,793	540
4	5,442	4,300	−1,142	5,757	315
5	6,423	5,050	−1,373	6,717	294
6	7,226	5,800	−1,426	7,667	441

a. Estimates by the Joint Committee on Internal Revenue Taxation.
b. $750 per capita exemption; flat $1,300 low-income allowance.
c. $750 per capita exemption plus $30 per capita credit; low-income allowance of $1,900 for married couples and $1,600 for single persons.

imum taxable levels, which were substantially below the poverty lines under the 1974 law, were raised above the estimated 1975 poverty lines for all family sizes except single persons (see table 2-4).

The adoption of the $30 per capita credit in 1975 was a compromise between those who wished to convert the entire exemption to a tax credit (computed by multiplying the value of the exemption by the first bracket rate or by some higher rate) and those who preferred to retain the exemption. The purpose of the credit was to reduce the tax benefits of the exemption increase for taxpayers in the higher income brackets.

The major objections to the tax credit as a complete replacement for the exemption are that it would be too generous for large families in the lower income classes and would narrow the tax differences among families of different sizes in the higher income classes. For example, if the exemption were converted to a $225 per capita credit, the minimum taxable level would be 35 percent higher than the estimated 1975 poverty level for a family of six and 15 percent higher for a single person.[12] In the 50 percent bracket, where the tax value of an exemption is $375, substitution of a $225 per capita credit for the exemption would reduce the spread between the tax paid by a family of six and that paid by a single person from $1,875 to $1,125.

12. The $225 credit would raise the minimum taxable level to $9,742 for a family of six and to $3,100 for a single person. As shown in table 2-4, the estimated poverty levels for 1975 are $7,226 and $2,850, respectively.

To avoid imposing heavier burdens on large families in the higher income classes, some propose that a tax credit be offered as an alternative to the exemption rather than as a substitute. By adjusting the tax rates, somewhat the same distribution of tax burdens by income class could be obtained without penalizing large families, but proponents of the credit are not persuaded that such an adjustment is politically feasible.

As prices continue to increase, some adjustment will be necessary to keep the minimum taxable levels from falling below the poverty lines. This objective can be achieved by increasing the exemptions, the low-income allowance, or the tax credit, or by a combination of the three. An analysis of three such possibilities, based on the assumption that the next adjustment of the minimum taxable levels is made after consumer prices rise 20 percent above average 1975 levels,[13] is summarized in tables 2-5 and 2-6. The possibilities are as follows:

1. Increase the per capita exemption from $750 to $1,000 and the low-income allowance to $2,600 for married couples and $2,300 for single persons, and repeal the $30 per capita credit. Under this method the minimum taxable levels for single people and families of five or more would be below the poverty lines but would exceed the poverty lines for families of two to four persons.

2. Retain the per capita exemption of $750 and the low-income allowance of $1,900 for married couples and $1,600 for single persons, and raise the per capita credit from $30 to $60. The credit, which would be in lieu of an increase in the per capita exemption, would raise the minimum taxable levels somewhat above the poverty lines for all families of two or more but would keep the minimum taxable level for single persons well below the poverty line.

3. Retain the low-income allowance of $1,900 for married couples and $1,600 for single persons, repeal the $30 per capita credit, and permit the taxpayer to elect a $225 per capita credit or a per capita exemption of $900, whichever is to his advantage. The optional tax credit would raise the minimum taxable levels well above the poverty levels for all families of two or more, but would keep the minimum taxable level for single persons below the poverty level. The increase in the exemption would provide tax reductions at all income levels.

The cost of increasing both the per capita exemption and the low-

---

13. Note (table 2-4) that the minimum taxable levels for families of two or more already exceed the 1975 poverty lines by 5 to 13 percent.

Table 2-5. Minimum Taxable Levels under the Present Individual Income Tax and under Various Exemption, Low-Income Allowance, and Tax Credit Plans Compared with Estimated Poverty Lines[a]

Dollars

Number in family	Poverty line[b]	Present law[c]		$1,000 per capita exemption; low-income allowance of $2,600 for married couples, $2,300 for single persons[d]		Raise per capita tax credit from $30 to $60[e]		$225 optional per capita tax credit[f]	
		Minimum taxable level	Difference	Minimum taxable level	Difference	Minimum taxable level	Difference	Minimum taxable level	Difference
1	3,420	2,564	−856	3,300	−120	2,779	−641	3,100	−320
2	4,164	3,829	−335	4,600	436	4,257	93	4,900	736
3	5,104	4,793	−311	5,600	496	5,417	313	6,189	1,085
4	6,530	5,757	−773	6,600	70	6,567	37	7,374	844
5	7,708	6,717	−991	7,600	−108	7,717	9	8,558	850
6	8,671	7,667	−1,004	8,600	−71	8,838	167	9,742	1,071

a. Poverty lines are estimated on the assumption of a 20 percent rise in consumer prices above 1975 average levels.
b. Based on 1975 estimates by the Joint Committee on Internal Revenue Taxation.
c. Per capita exemption of $750 and per capita credit of $30; low-income allowance of $1,900 for married couples and $1,600 for single persons.
d. Assumes repeal of the $30 per capita credit.
e. Assumes retention of the $750 per capita exemption and low-income allowance of $1,900 for married couples and $1,600 for single persons.
f. Taxpayer is allowed to use the credit or a $900 per capita exemption, whichever is to his advantage; assumes low-income allowance of $1,900 for married couples and $1,600 for single persons.

Table 2-6. Revenue and Distributional Effects of Various Individual
Income Tax Exemption, Low-Income Allowance, and Tax Credit Plans,
by Adjusted Gross Income Class, 1976
Income classes in thousands of dollars

Revenue change and adjusted gross income class	*$1,000 per capita exemption; low-income allowance of $2,600 for married couples, $2,300 for single persons*	*Raise per capita tax credit from $30 to $60*	*$900 per capita exemption or $225 optional per capita tax credit*
Revenue change (millions of dollars)	−8,300	−5,100	−5,100
Percentage distribution of revenue change			
0–3	0.4	0.5	0.8
3–5	7.6	3.9	7.2
5–10	30.0	19.8	29.5
10–15	21.1	27.5	32.6
15–20	13.7	22.1	13.8
20–25	9.3	12.3	4.4
25–50	12.9	11.5	7.8
50–100	3.9	1.9	3.0
100–200	0.9	0.4	0.8
200–500	0.2	0.1	0.1
500–1,000	*	*	*
1,000 and over	*	*	*
All classes[a]	100.0	100.0	100.0
Percentage change in tax liabilities			
0–3	−86.9	−64.2	−91.8
3–5	−53.9	−17.4	−31.3
5–10	−22.5	−9.3	−13.5
10–15	−8.7	−7.0	−8.2
15–20	−4.8	−4.8	−3.0
20–25	−4.2	−3.4	−1.2
25–50	−3.5	−2.0	−1.3
50–100	−2.1	−0.6	−1.0
100–200	−1.0	−0.2	−0.5
200–500	−0.4	−0.1	−0.2
500–1,000	−0.2	*	−0.1
1,000 and over	*	*	*
All classes[a]	−6.2	−3.9	−3.8

Source: Brookings 1972 tax file, projected to 1976. Figures are rounded. For explanation of the alternative plans, see notes, table 2-5.
* Less than 0.05 percent.
a. Includes negative incomes not shown separately.

income allowance is higher—$8 billion a year—than the cost of the other plans—roughly $5 billion a year. All three plans would concentrate the relief mainly in the lower and middle income classes, with the tax credit somewhat less favorable to the higher income classes.

Income Splitting and the Treatment of Two-Earner Married Couples

Income splitting is the method used to distinguish the tax rates applying to the income of single persons from those for married couples. It was adopted in the United States because eight states had community property laws that treated a couple's income as if it were owned equally by the husband and wife. These property arrangements were recognized by the Supreme Court for federal income tax purposes. Immediately after World War II, a number of other states enacted community property laws for the sole purpose of obtaining the advantage of income splitting for their residents. To avoid the disruption of property arrangements and to equalize the taxes paid by married couples living in different states, Congress in 1948 extended the privilege of income splitting for tax purposes to all married couples.

Under the income-splitting provision, the tax of a married couple is computed as if each spouse received half the total income of the couple. The effect is to double the width of the tax brackets and thus reduce progression in the tax rates for many married couples.[14] Under present tax rates, the tax advantage of the double brackets rises from $5 for married couples with taxable income of $1,000 to $14,510 for couples with taxable income of $200,000 or more. In percentage terms, the advantage reaches a maximum of about 30 percent at the $28,000 level. The revenue loss amounts to about $32 billion a year,[15] 94 percent of which is attributed to taxpayers with incomes above $10,000.

14. Married couples filing separate returns are required to use the old single-person rate schedule, whose tax brackets are half as wide as the brackets for couples filing joint returns. The effect of income splitting on tax liabilities is greatest for couples with only one income earner. It becomes less and less for two-earner families as the incomes of the two members come closer together and disappears entirely for couples with equal separate incomes.

15. This includes the revenue effect of the special tax rates for heads of households and other single persons that have been enacted because of income splitting (see below).

The income-splitting device achieved its objective of geographic tax equality for married couples. The states that had adopted community property laws for tax reasons alone repealed them almost immediately. Problems created by such income-splitting arrangements as family partnerships and gifts from one spouse to the other became less acute and are rarely mentioned today. The vast majority of married couples in this country file joint returns and are spared the complications of dividing their incomes, exemptions, and deductions on separate returns. In addition, the tax paid by two single people with separate incomes was the same under the original income-splitting arrangements before and after marriage.

However, these advantages were purchased at a heavy cost in equity as well as in revenue terms. Since income splitting is confined to married couples, those who are not married do not benefit from the provision, even though they may have similar family responsibilities. It was soon found that a sharp dividing line cannot be drawn on the basis of marital status alone. As a result, Congress has moved the tax burdens of single persons closer to those of married couples on several occasions since 1948, most recently in 1969. Widows and widowers with children are now permitted to split their incomes for two years after the death of the spouse; half the advantage of joint returns is given to single persons with children or other dependents or who maintain a separate household for their parents; and single persons who are not heads of households are allowed to use a rate schedule with tax liabilities that never exceed by more than 20 percent the liabilities for married couples filing joint returns. These modifications mean that taxpayers must choose from among four different sets of tax rates when figuring their tax liabilities each April 15.

With the reduction in tax rates for single persons, it is now possible for two single people to be subject to higher taxes after than before marriage. For example, the total tax paid by two single people each with an income of $15,000 (and personal deductions of 17 percent of income) is $5,038 under the 1975 law. If they marry, their taxes are raised by $370, or 7 percent. This so-called "penalty on marriage" rises to a maximum of 18 percent for people with separate incomes of $30,000 each.

Clearly it is difficult to arrive at a satisfactory balance between the tax liabilities of single persons and of families through modifications of the tax rate schedules. One solution is to equalize the tax rates for all tax units with the same *taxable* income, and to make allowances for family size and other family characteristics through exemptions and deductions. The tax rates can be equalized either by doubling the width of the tax brackets used by single persons or by halving the tax brackets for married couples.[16] The former device would extend the rate advantages of income splitting to single persons and lose an additional $3.8 billion of revenue a year; the latter would keep the device of income splitting for married couples (so that geographic equality is maintained) but would eliminate the rate advantages and recapture the annual revenue loss of $32 billion. Tax rates could of course be reduced to offset part or all of the increased tax burden imposed on married couples.

But equalizing the tax rates of single people and married couples would fail to distinguish between married couples with one earner and those with two earners and would also raise the marriage penalty on the two-earner couple. The tax laws were given their present form at a time when it was considered normal for the husband to work and the wife to remain at home. At present, the majority of married couples are both earners, and it is no longer appropriate to treat the one-earner couple as the norm.

The tax provisions applying to one- and two-earner couples are identical; hence, if they have the same money income, the same number of exemptions, and the same deductions, they pay the same tax. This gives the wrong tax result, because the married couple with one spouse working has more taxpaying ability than the married couple with two spouses working. The spouse who does not work produces "income" while he or she is at home, but the income so produced is in the form of services to the family that cannot be evaluated in money terms and therefore cannot be taxed. If both spouses work, the type of service performed by the nonworking spouse may be performed by a paid domestic servant; even if they get along without a domestic servant, their expenditures on clothing, laundry, and food are generally higher. It is not fair to tax the combined earnings of the two spouses in full because some part of the earnings is absorbed in meeting these extra expenses. Furthermore, the heavy tax on the earnings of the second spouse discourages people who might otherwise be working from obtaining employment.

16. Under both alternatives, the head-of-household schedule and the special rates for single persons would be eliminated.

It has been suggested that the problem could be resolved by eliminating income splitting and reducing the tax rates, but this solution would restore all the problems of the pre-1948 arrangements. Income splitting has the great merit that married couples with the same taxable income pay the same tax regardless of how their income is split between them. Two-earner couples are treated unfairly under income splitting, not because a system based on the combined income of married couples is unfair, but because the taxable income of the one-earner couple is understated in that it does not include the value of services provided by the spouse who stays at home. Elimination of income splitting would not greatly alter the marginal tax rates on the earnings of two-earner married couples and would therefore have little incentive effect.

A modest effort was made to provide some relief for the two-earner couple through a special deduction for child care expenses, which was adopted in 1954 and liberalized in 1964, 1971, and 1975. Under the present provision, married couples with both working full time and single persons may deduct up to $200 a month for the care of one child, $300 a month for two children, and $400 a month for three or more children. The deduction is reduced by fifty cents for each dollar of adjusted gross income above $35,000 a year. The deduction, which was used on 1,569,000 returns in 1972, amounted to only $1.1 billion and probably had a tax value of $275 million. Although the deduction reduces some of the tax inequity between one- and two-earner married couples, it does nothing for those who have no children. In addition, some have reservations about the child care deduction, claiming that the tax laws should be neutral toward earners whether or not they have children.

It is obviously impossible to calculate the exact amount by which the taxable income of the two-earner couple is overstated as compared with that of the one-earner couple. Two devices have been proposed from time to time to adjust the taxable income of the two-earner couple, either as a substitute for the child care deduction or as a supplement: the first is a deduction and the second is a tax credit, both based on the earned income of the spouse with the lower earnings. The major difference is that the tax value of an exempted dollar of earnings by the lower earner rises as the marginal rate increases, whereas the credit provides the same tax reduction per dollar of earnings in all taxable income classes. The deduction makes the adjustment by refining gross income in arriving at taxable income, but some favor the credit to avoid giving a larger relative tax advantage to wealthier couples.

Since the difference in taxpaying ability between one-earner and two-earner couples and the effects of the tax rates on the incentives of the second spouse are not inconsequential, the special deduction or credit must be significant to do any good. It might also taper off for taxpayers with high earned income, because the higher costs incurred and the value of household services lost by the two-earner couple do not continue to rise with income indefinitely. For example, working couples might be given a special deduction of 25 percent of the earnings of the spouse with the lower earnings, up to a maximum of $2,500; or they might be given a tax credit of 10 percent of the earnings of the spouse with the lower earnings, up to a maximum of $1,000. With such a generous deduction or tax credit, the marriage penalty would be eliminated for people with separate earnings up to about $20,000 each and the child care deduction could be reduced substantially or eliminated entirely.

Table 2-7 shows the revenue implications, by income class, of the revisions in income splitting and the allowances for two-earner couples. If the tax rate advantages of married couples under income splitting were removed completely, revenues would be increased by $32 billion a year. On the other hand, if the full rate advantages of income splitting were extended to single persons, revenues would be reduced by almost $4 billion a year. Adoption of the credit or deduction for two-earner married couples would cost $6 billion to $9 billion a year. Extension of the married couples' rates to single persons would have a major effect on tax liabilities in the lowest income classes, where single persons are concentrated; most of the effect of the proposal to eliminate the rate advantages of income splitting would be in the classes with income between $10,000 and $50,000. With appropriate rate adjustments, the net effect of such revisions would be to redistribute tax burdens between single persons and married couples and between one- and two-earner couples.

Correcting Tax Liabilities for Inflation

Increasing concern has been expressed about the effects of income tax progressivity on the burden of taxpayers during periods of inflation. As money income rises, the top portion of a taxpayer's income

Table 2-7. Revenue Effects of Changes in Income Splitting and Allowances for Two-Earner Married Couples, by Adjusted Gross Income Class, 1976

Income classes in thousands of dollars

Revenue change and adjusted gross income class	Extend rate advantages of income splitting to single persons			Eliminate rate advantages of income splitting for married couples		
	No special deduction for married couples	With special deduction of 25 percent of earnings of spouse with lower earnings[a]	With special tax credit of 10 percent of earnings of spouse with lower earnings[b]	No special deduction for married couples	With special deduction of 25 percent of earnings of spouse with lower earnings[a]	With special tax credit of 10 percent of earnings of spouse with lower earnings[b]
Revenue change (millions of dollars)	−3,800	−9,400	−12,800	32,000	24,100	23,000
Percentage distribution of revenue change						
0–3	0.8	0.3	0.2	*	*	*
3–5	7.5	3.1	2.3	*	*	*
5–10	30.7	14.5	12.6	1.8	1.5	0.6
10–15	21.8	17.8	19.6	8.7	7.1	4.8
15–20	16.6	22.3	25.4	16.9	13.9	12.1
20–25	7.1	17.5	19.1	18.3	15.7	16.0
25–50	9.3	18.9	17.1	36.6	39.8	43.0
50–100	3.8	4.0	2.6	12.8	15.9	17.0
100–200	1.6	1.2	0.8	3.8	4.8	5.1
200–500	0.7	0.4	0.3	0.8	1.1	1.1
500–1,000	0.1	0.1	*	0.1	0.1	0.1
1,000 and over	*	*	*	*	*	*ᵢ
All classes[c]	100.0	100.0	100.0	100.0	100.0	100.0
Percentage change in tax liabilities						
0–3	−68.2	−68.2	−68.4	*	*	−0.2
3–5	−24.7	−25.1	−25.4	0.5	*	−0.3
5–10	−10.7	−12.5	−14.6	5.3	3.2	1.3
10–15	−4.2	−8.4	−12.6	13.9	8.6	5.5
15–20	−2.7	−8.9	−13.8	22.9	14.2	11.8
20–25	−1.5	−8.9	−13.3	31.7	20.5	19.9
25–50	−1.2	−5.9	−7.2	38.7	31.7	32.6
50–100	−1.0	−2.5	−2.2	26.9	25.3	25.7
100–200	−0.8	−1.5	−1.3	16.1	15.4	15.6
200–500	−0.8	−1.1	−1.0	7.6	7.3	7.4
500–1,000	−0.5	−0.6	−0.5	3.1	3.0	3.0
1,000 and over	−0.1	−0.2	−0.2	1.0	0.9	0.9
All classes[c]	−2.9	−7.1	−9.6	24.0	18.1	17.3

Source: Brookings 1972 tax file, projected to 1976. Figures are rounded.
* Less than 0.05 percent.
a. Assuming maximum deduction of $2,500.
b. Assuming maximum tax credit of $1,000.
c. Includes negative incomes not shown separately.

is pushed into higher tax brackets, with the result that the average effective rate rises even if income only keeps pace with inflation. A number of countries with high rates of inflation adjust income tax exemptions and tax rate brackets to eliminate this effect.[17] Until re-

17. The method is to raise the exemptions and the limits of each tax rate bracket annually by the inflation rate; the rates remain unchanged. Such adjustments have been made for a number of years in Brazil and Israel. Canada, where the rate of inflation has been closer to that in the United States, adopted such procedures effective for the year 1974.

Table 2-8. Effect of Inflation on Individual Income Tax Liabilities
Percent

Assumed inflation rate	Total per capita income growth[a]	Effective rates[b]		Increase in effective rates	Reduction in disposable income caused by inflation
		Noninflationary period[a]	Inflationary period		
		After two-year inflation			
5	9	13.09	13.81	5.50	0.83
10	14	13.09	14.53	11.00	1.66
15	19	13.09	15.24	16.42	2.47
		After five-year inflation			
5	9	14.00	15.97	14.07	2.29
10	14	14.00	18.25	30.36	4.94
15	19	14.00	20.86	49.00	7.98

Source: Calculations are based on the Brookings 1972 tax file, projected to 1976.
a. Assumes real income growth of 3 percent a year per capita and average price increases of 1 percent a year in the noninflationary period.
b. Individual income tax liabilities under the 1975 tax law as a percent of adjusted gross income reported on federal individual income tax returns.

cently, when the rate of inflation accelerated, the problem received no attention in the United States.

The effect of inflation (with the type of individual income tax structure now in effect in the United States) is illustrated in the calculations summarized in table 2-8. It was assumed that per capita income would grow at 4 percent a year in a noninflationary period, beginning in 1976.[18] Per capita incomes were then increased 5, 10, and 15 percent a year for inflation, yielding, respectively, total annual increases of 9, 14, and 19 percent in per capita incomes. The effective tax rates were calculated for all persons filing tax returns after two years and five years of such inflation rates and then compared with the effective rates in the noninflationary period. The difference between the two represents the increase in the individual income tax burden resulting from the inflation.

The effect is large if inflation proceeds at a relatively high rate for a long period of time. For example, with an inflation rate of 10 percent a year, individual income tax liabilities at the end of the two years are, on the average, 11 percent higher than they would have

18. This is the sum of 3 percent annual growth in productivity and a minimum allowance of 1 percent for the gradual increase in the general price level that occurs during a noninflationary period.

been in the noninflationary period, while disposable income is less than 2 percent lower. If the 10 percent inflation lasts for five years, the increase in tax liabilities caused by the inflation is 30 percent and the reduction in disposable income is almost 5 percent.

There are a number of arguments for adjusting the exemptions and the tax brackets for inflation. In the first place, the increased income tax collections are unintended by-products of inflation. Without adjustment, government revenues increase faster than incomes and the size of the public sector grows faster in relation to the rest of the economy than it would in a noninflationary situation. Second, the increased burdens may produce real hardships for taxpayers, particularly for those who are at or near the poverty level. Third, the distribution of the increased tax burden by income level does not follow a pattern selected by Congress but depends on the progressivity of the income tax and the rate of inflation.

On the other hand, correction for inflation would reduce the effectiveness of the income tax as a built-in stabilizer during an inflationary period. The rise in tax yields automatically moderates the growth in aggregate demand and thus contributes to stabilization.[19] Experience has shown that it is virtually impossible to increase federal tax rates in peacetime. Consequently, if the inflation adjustment turns out to be too large for stabilization reasons, it will be difficult in practice to recover the loss in revenue by discretionary increases in tax rates. Moreover, if the tax revenue flow is considered too large, Congress always has the option of reducing tax rates or increasing exemptions —as it did in 1969 and 1975.

Table 2-9 shows the tax liabilities that might result from an inflation-adjusted individual income tax for a family of four with selected income ranging from $8,000 to $100,000. It is assumed that the rate of inflation is 10 percent a year for periods of two years and five years. The tax liabilities under present law are compared with those resulting from the application of two methods of correcting for inflation. Method A would increase the exemptions, the per capita tax credit,

19. In the long run, the level of federal expenditures is a function of the yield of the tax system. In the short run, however, the yield of the individual income tax during an inflationary period outstrips the rise in expenditures even though some of the expenditures tend to escalate in line with the rise in the price level. See Barry M. Blechman, Edward M. Gramlich, and Robert W. Hartman, *Setting National Priorities: The 1976 Budget* (Brookings Institution, 1975), pp. 210–26.

Table 2-9. Comparison of Tax Liabilities after Two-Year and Five-Year Periods of 10 Percent Inflation a Year under the 1975 Tax Law, and Two Methods of Correcting for Inflation, Married Couples with Two Children, by Selected Income

Income (dollars)	Tax liability[a] (dollars)			Percentage change from tax liability under present law[b]	
	1975 law[c]	Method A[d]	Method B[e]	Method A[d]	Method B[e]
	After two-year inflation				
8,000	648	420	432	−35.3	−33.3
10,000	1,078	858	887	−20.5	−17.7
12,000	1,491	1,285	1,327	−13.8	−11.0
15,000	2,156	1,910	1,990	−11.4	−7.7
20,000	3,444	3,073	3,242	−10.8	−5.9
25,000	4,934	4,392	4,707	−11.0	−4.6
50,000	15,548	13,727	15,206	−11.7	−2.2
100,000	40,655	38,646	40,314	−4.9	−0.8
	After five-year inflation				
8,000	1,202	559	615	−53.5	−48.8
10,000	1,781	1,142	1,234	−35.9	−30.7
12,000	2,400	1,711	1,893	−28.7	−21.2
15,000	3,434	2,543	2,872	−26.0	−16.4
20,000	5,455	4,091	4,795	−25.0	−12.1
25,000	7,923	5,846	7,135	−26.2	−9.9
50,000	23,858	18,271	22,869	−23.4	−4.2
100,000	57,276	51,439	56,286	−10.2	−1.7

a. Tax liabilities were computed on the assumptions that all income is earned and that the taxpayer uses the low-income allowance of $1,900 or 17 percent of income, whichever is larger.

b. Figures are rounded.

c. Refers to the rates, exemptions, and credits enacted under the Tax Reduction Act of 1975.

d. Would increase the exemptions, the low-income allowance, the per capita tax credit, the refundable earned-income credit, and the rate bracket limits by the percentage of inflation.

e. Would increase the exemptions, the low-income allowance, the per capita tax credit, and the refundable earned-income credit by the percentage of inflation, but would not alter the rate bracket limits.

the low-income allowance,[20] the limits for the earned-income credit, and the bracket limits by the percentage of inflation. This would completely remove the taxpayers' loss of income resulting from the application of the progressive income tax to the inflated incomes.[21] In Method B the inflation adjustment is made for the exemptions, the

20. The limit on the maximum standard deductions would also be raised by the inflation percentage, but this does not apply to the illustration in table 2-9 because it is assumed that all taxpayers itemize deductions of 17 percent of their income.

21. In principle, to remove the effect of inflation completely would require correcting all absolute income limits in the tax law—for example, the limit on deductible health insurance premiums, the $100 floor on deductions for casualty losses, and the income limit for the child care deduction. In practice, the effects of these limits are much less significant than the effects of the fixed dollar amounts for the exemptions, the low-income allowance, the two credits, and the rate bracket limits.

two credits, and the low-income allowance, but not for the rate brackets.

If the full correction were used (Method A), the tax after a five-year period of inflation would be adjusted downward by 53 percent at the $8,000 income level, 26 percent at $15,000, 26 percent at $25,000, and 10 percent at $100,000. If the correction were confined to the exemptions, the credits, and the low-income allowance (Method B), the downward adjustment would be 49 percent at the $8,000 level, 16 percent at $15,000, 10 percent at $25,000, and 2 percent at $100,000. In effect, Method B would correct almost fully for the inflation at the $8,000 level, about 38 percent at a level as high as $25,000, and only 11 percent at $100,000.

These calculations indicate that the additional income tax burden imposed by inflation is heaviest in relative terms at and near the exemption levels and declines as incomes rise. An annual or periodic adjustment of the exemptions, the credits, and the low-income allowance by the rate of inflation (Method B) would therefore eliminate a major share of the tax hardship resulting from the inflation. The best insurance against this and other hardships caused by inflation would of course be to avoid the inflation in the first place.

Rate Adjustments

Most of the tax revisions discussed in this and the following chapters would increase tax revenues, some by substantial amounts. While part of these revenues might be used to pay for new federal expenditure programs, the largest share should probably be returned to the taxpayers in reduced rates. The effects of the present marginal rates on a substantially more comprehensive tax base might seriously impair economic incentives. At present, tax rate schedules rise to a maximum of 70 percent, but for earned income graduation is cut off at 50 percent.

The rate reductions do not have to be distributed in accordance with a standard or uniform formula. In fact, if the revisions tend to place a heavier burden on some income classes than on others, more generous rate reductions for the overburdened classes might be needed. It is nevertheless instructive to examine the ways in which the entire rate schedule can be modified by relatively simple devices to achieve various objectives. These devices fall into three categories.

First, taxes might be raised or lowered by a positive or negative surcharge; that is, a flat percentage increase or decrease in all tax liabilities. This type of adjustment is highly progressive when tax rates are raised and regressive when they are lowered. For example, a 10 percent change in tax liabilities would raise or lower the first bracket rate of 14 percent by 1.4 percentage points and the top bracket rate of 70 percent by 7 percentage points, with corresponding changes in all other rates. Taxable income after taxes would be raised or lowered by 23.3 percent in the top bracket (7 divided by 30); by contrast, the change in the first bracket would be minimal, 1.6 percent (1.4 divided by 86). Congress adopted the surcharge to increase taxes during the Korean and Vietnam wars,[22] but it has never used this device to lower taxes.

Second, the rate of graduation could be kept the same by a uniform adjustment in all tax rates. For example, a 2 percentage point reduction across the board would cut the 14 percent rate to 12 percent and the 70 percent rate to 68 percent. Under this method, the tax change would amount to the same percentage of taxable income in all income classes. On an after-tax basis, it would also be progressive when the rates were raised and regressive when the rates were lowered, but the degree of change in either direction (2.3 percent in the first bracket and 6.7 percent in the top bracket) would be relatively small compared with the surcharge method.

Third, the rates could be adjusted so as to raise or lower the after-tax income in each rate bracket by the same proportion. In the first bracket 86 percent of taxable income is left after tax, whereas in the top bracket 30 percent is left after tax. A 3 percent change in after-tax taxable income would change the 14 percent rate by 2.58 percentage points (3 percent of 86 percent) and the 70 percent rate by 0.9 percentage point (3 percent of 30 percent). Clearly, however, the distribution of taxable income after tax would remain unchanged.

The three methods have about the same effect on revenues if the surcharge is 10 percent, the across-the-board rate change is 2 percentage points, and the change in taxable income after tax is 3 per-

---

22. During the Korean War, when the regular rates reached a maximum of 91 percent, a basic surcharge of 11.75 percent was adopted, but the amount of the surcharge was limited to no more than 9 percent of taxable income after tax. As a result, the top bracket rate was increased to only 92 percent. During the Vietnam War, when the regular top bracket rate was 70 percent, a 10 percent surcharge was applied across the board. This raised the top bracket rate to 77 percent.

Table 2-10. Revenue Effects of Three Methods of Adjusting Tax Rates, 1976
Income classes in thousands of dollars

Revenue change and adjusted gross income class	10 percent surcharge	2 percentage point change in all rates	3 percent change in taxable income after tax
Revenue change			
(billions of dollars)	13.3	12.4	14.6
Percentage distribution of revenue change			
0–3	*	0.1	0.1
3–5	0.8	1.4	1.6
5–10	8.1	11.3	12.2
10–15	15.1	19.2	20.4
15–20	17.8	20.8	21.6
20–25	13.9	15.0	15.3
25–50	22.8	20.7	20.1
50–100	11.5	7.1	5.9
100–200	5.7	2.7	1.9
200–500	2.6	1.0	0.6
500–1,000	0.7	0.3	0.1
1,000 and over	0.8	0.3	0.1
All classes	100.0	100.0	100.0
Percentage change in tax liabilities			
0–3	10.0	25.7	35.2
3–5	10.0	15.7	20.4
5–10	10.0	13.1	16.6
10–15	10.0	11.9	14.9
15–20	10.0	10.9	13.4
20–25	10.0	10.1	12.1
25–50	10.0	8.5	9.7
50–100	10.0	5.8	5.7
100–200	10.0	4.5	3.7
200–500	10.0	3.7	2.5
500–1,000	10.0	3.2	1.8
1,000 and over	10.0	3.0	1.5
All classes	10.0	9.3	11.0

Source: Brookings 1972 tax file, projected to 1976. The calculations were made for reductions in tax rates; the effect of increasing tax rates would be roughly the same.
* Less than 0.05 percent.

cent. At 1976 income levels the amounts are about $13.5 billion a year for the surcharge, $12.5 billion for the percentage-point method, and $14.5 billion for the after-tax adjustment method. Of the total tax change, 44 percent would be concentrated in the income classes above $25,000 under the surcharge method, 32 percent under the percentage-point method, and 29 percent under the after-tax adjustment method (see table 2-10).

CHAPTER THREE

Treatment of Investment and Business Income

CAPITAL GAINS, interest, dividends, profits, and rents and royalties are all taxable under both the individual and the corporation income taxes, and major problems are created by the way the different kinds of investment and business income are currently treated.

Capital Gains and Losses

Originally taxed as ordinary income, profits on the sale of capital assets (such as stocks, bonds, and real estate) have since 1921 for individuals and since 1942 for corporations been subject to preferential tax rates.[1] At the present time only one-half of the capital gain on an asset held over six months—defined as a long-term capital gain

---

1. The distinction between capital assets and other assets and that between ordinary income and capital gains income are among the most complex in federal income tax law. These are discussed by Richard Goode, *The Individual Income Tax,* revised edition (Brookings Institution, 1975), chapter 8; Boris I. Bittker and Lawrence M. Stone, *Federal Income, Estate and Gift Taxation,* fourth edition (Little, Brown, 1972), chapter 6; and Stanley S. Surrey, William C. Warren, Paul R. McDaniel, and Hugh J. Ault, *Federal Income Taxation, Cases and Materials* (Foundation Press, 1972), chapter 5.

—is included in taxable income. This means that effective federal income tax rates on most long-term capital gains now range from 7 percent to 35 percent while other kinds of income and short-term capital gains are taxed at rates of 14 to 70 percent. The first $50,000 of long-term gains are subject to a maximum, or "alternative," tax rate of 25 percent.[2]

Capital gains are taxable only when realized by sale or exchange. As a consequence, investors who hold onto their assets can increase their wealth by the full amount of any accrued capital gains without paying tax while other taxpayers can save only the after-tax amounts of whatever ordinary income they receive. Moreover, all capital gains accrued on assets transferred at the death of the owner are exempt from income tax, and those that are transferred by gift are subject to tax only if the donee sells them before his death.

This preferential tax treatment applies to a form of income that is both important in the aggregate and highly concentrated in the upper income groups. It has been estimated, for example, that between 1948 and 1964 capital gains accrued at an average rate of $40 billion a year, which is more than twice the rate at which families saved all other kinds of income during the same period. Some 60 percent of those gains accrued on corporate stock, 27 percent on nonfarm residential real estate, and 13 percent on farm real estate. The high concentration of this kind of wealth is indicated by the fact that the top 2 percent of all income receivers in 1962—those with income of $25,000 or more—are estimated to have received 11 percent of total ordinary income in that year but over 50 percent of all capital gains accruing between 1960 and 1964.[3]

Arriving at an equitable and economically balanced method of taxing capital gains and losses, then, is a policy problem of major

2. Under certain circumstances, the law also requires both the subtraction of one-half of all long-term gains from any salary amounts that would otherwise qualify for the maximum 50 percent tax rate on earned income and the addition of these gains to the preferential income base subject to the 10 percent minimum tax. This means that the effective tax rate on long-term capital gains may be as high as 36.5 percent for investors not eligible for the maximum tax rate on earned income and 45.5 percent for those who are. The minimum income tax provisions are discussed later in this chapter.

3. Capital gains are still heavily concentrated in the higher income classes. In 1972, the latest year for which data are available, tax returns reporting incomes of $25,000 or more accounted for 62 percent of the capital gains and only 17 percent of ordinary income.

proportions, with implications for both the growth and the distribution of society's total income and wealth. In the eyes of many, equity demands that capital gains be treated in exactly the same way as other kinds of income, but in practice this introduces a complex set of requirements. Annual evaluations of accrued capital gains would have to be made, with suitable adjustments for the burdens of any separate taxes on retained corporate profits and possibly also for changes in the general price level. Whether these changes would make tax compliance more or less difficult is hard to predict. Much would be gained by eliminating all taxpayer incentives to convert ordinary income into capital gains form, but annual asset valuations, or periodic valuations combined with a comprehensive income-averaging system for federal taxpayers, would complicate the tax affairs of many. Moreover, taxpayers owning difficult-to-value assets infrequently traded on the open market could be faced with serious liquidity problems and a high degree of uncertainty about their proper tax liabilities. Owners of family farms and businesses with few other assets would be especially hard pressed to pay taxes on their accrued capital gains, and owners of special assets with unique features would inevitably be uncertain, even suspicious, about the values placed on those assets for tax purposes.

Nevertheless, accrual taxation would not be at all difficult for assets, such as corporate shares, that are traded regularly on organized exchanges. Less frequently traded assets, such as real estate, could be added as soon as uniform, high-quality property assessment standards, desirable in their own right for local tax purposes, were established on a nationwide basis. Thus for a substantial proportion of all capital gains accrual taxation is by no means as farfetched a proposal as many would like to believe. Not the least of its accomplishments, it has been estimated, would be the elimination of one-half to two-thirds of the pages required to set forth the federal income tax law and its accompanying regulations. With this prospect in sight, it might also be a good time to get rid of many of the economic distortions caused by the federal corporation profits tax. These possibilities are discussed in the next chapter.

Taxation of capital gains on a realization basis eliminates some of the practical problems of an accrual system but creates others. A high tax on the sale of capital assets tends to discourage such transactions and can effectively lock many investors into their existing portfolios to the detriment of a flexible and responsive capital market. Taxation only at realization also introduces the inequity of allowing investors to use capital losses to offset taxes currently due on other kinds of income while deferring the payment of taxes on accrued capital gains. To prevent huge revenue losses, taxpayers are only permitted to offset their net capital losses (after the 50 percent exclusion for long-term losses) against $1,000 of ordinary income in the year of realization and to carry over such losses against capital gains and $1,000 of other income in subsequent years until they are used up. Dealing with the distortions arising from the realization principle by applying low preferential rates to capital gains and by restricting the offset of capital losses against ordinary income raises serious questions of equity and risks the diversion of economic activity from more to less productive areas.

Little wonder, then, that the ideal form of capital gains taxation is elusive. Many specific reform proposals have been made, some to tighten and others to loosen existing provisions.

Assets Transferred by Gift, Bequest, or Donation

Many capital gains currently escape taxation completely when assets are bequeathed at the death of the owner, donated to charity, or transferred by gift. Consider a person with a capital asset bought years ago for $2,000 and now worth $10,000. If he gives it to an eligible philanthropic organization, he can deduct the full $10,000 in computing his taxable income for the year and pay no tax at all on the accrued $8,000 capital gain. If he gives it to his child, he owes no tax on the gain at the time of the gift. Furthermore, the child becomes taxable on the $8,000 increment only if and when he sells the asset. If the original owner holds the asset until his death and bequeaths it to his child, the latter will take $10,000 as his own cost basis (assuming that to be the fair market value at the date of death) and the $8,000 capital gain will be taxable to neither parent nor child.

Such tax avoidance could be prevented by requiring what are called "constructive realizations" for income tax purposes whenever assets are transferred in the ways just described. In each case the original owner would then pay tax on the $8,000 accrued gain just as if he had sold the asset. Subsequently, in the case of gift, the donee would take a cost basis of $10,000 (rather than the $2,000 he now can use); and in the case of bequest, the decedent's income tax on the $8,000 gain would be deducted from the taxable value of his estate (as is any other debt).

Constructive realization for capital gains would improve tax equity, and also reduce the lock-in effect that is particularly strong among older investors, since it would remove the possibility of escaping capital gains taxes entirely by holding onto assets. The effect on revenue of a change in this policy would be determined to some extent by how much portfolio activity was induced by the new tax. During the period of transition to the new system, the selection of the base to which the constructive realization would be applied would be a major determinant of the revenue yield. Some advocates of the change would make all capital gains subject to the new provision regardless of when they accrued, while others would restrict the base to gains accruing after enactment of the law. The latter decision would provide a small but growing revenue gain for the Treasury, though one that could not in the short run be predicted with confidence.[4]

A decision to apply constructive realization to estimated gains that will have accrued on 1976 gifts and bequests would produce a revenue increase of $2.2 billion (see table 3-1).

Adjusting the Length of the Holding Period

The six-month holding period that separates short- from long-term gains has been criticized as being both too long and too short. Investor groups argue that the holding period should be reduced to three months or eliminated entirely. They contend that such a change would increase the number of security transactions and thus raise capital gains tax revenues. Others argue that in an annual income tax there is no equitable basis for reducing the tax rate on incomes earned in less than one year. On the assumption that there would be little change in the number of transactions, lengthening the holding period from six months to one year would raise 1976 tax revenues by $900 million a year (table 3-1).

---

4. To avoid the need for tracing the cost of small amounts of personal assets like jewelry, furniture, and paintings, an exemption of the first $2,000 or $5,000 of capital asset transfers might be needed. Some have also suggested, though for different reasons, an exemption of $25,000 of constructively realized gains on personal residences.

Table 3-1. Revenue Effects of Various Capital Gains Tax Revisions, by Adjusted Gross Income Class, 1976

Income classes in thousands of dollars

Revenue change and adjusted gross income class	Constructive realization of gains from gift and at death	Lengthen holding period from 6 to 12 months	Reduce inclusion percentage from 50 to 25 percent	Taxation at regular rates	
				Realized gains only	Realized and constructively realized gains
Revenue change (millions of dollars)	2,200	900	−2,300	6,200	11,100
	Percentage distribution of revenue change				
0–3	*	*	*	0.1	0.1
3–5	2.5	0.1	0.4	0.6	1.5
5–10	7.4	4.0	3.1	3.0	5.4
10–15	8.1	2.1	4.2	3.7	6.0
15–20	5.6	6.1	6.4	6.2	6.1
20–25	11.0	3.6	5.3	4.8	7.7
25–50	28.3	17.3	16.9	15.8	21.0
50–100	11.2	16.9	19.3	18.3	15.1
100–200	11.0	16.7	16.4	16.7	13.9
200–500	7.0	15.7	13.3	13.5	10.4
500–1,000	3.1	7.6	5.9	6.3	4.7
1,000 and over	4.9	9.8	8.9	10.9	8.0
All classes[a]	100.0	100.0	100.0	100.0	100.0
	Percentage change in tax liabilities				
0–3	2.2	0.7	*	15.6[b]	26.0[b]
3–5	4.7	0.1	−0.7	3.0	14.4
5–10	1.5	0.3	−0.6	1.7	5.4
10–15	0.9	0.1	−0.5	1.2	3.3
15–20	0.5	0.2	−0.6	1.6	2.8
20–25	1.3	0.2	−0.7	1.6	4.6
25–50	2.1	0.5	−1.3	3.2	7.6
50–100	1.6	1.0	−2.9	7.5	10.9
100–200	3.2	1.9	−5.0	13.6	20.2
200–500	4.4	3.9	−8.8	24.0	32.8
500–1,000	6.9	6.9	−14.1	40.1	53.7
1,000 and over	9.6	7.7	−18.6	60.8	79.5
All classes[a]	1.7	0.7	−1.7	4.7	8.3

Source: Brookings 1972 tax file, projected to 1976. Figures are rounded.
* Less than 0.05 percent.
a. Includes negative incomes not shown separately.
b. Percent increase in tax is unusually high because many persons with large incomes have tax shelters that reduce their adjusted gross income to less than $3,000 and pay virtually no individual income tax.

Special Inflation Adjustments

Whenever the general price level changes significantly, only a portion of nominal capital gains represents real income. Consider a capital asset bought for $10,000 and sold five years later for $15,000. Under current law the owner would be taxable on a long-term gain of $2,500 even though if prices had risen by 50 percent over the five years he would have realized no real gain at all. To correct for inflation, it would be necessary to compute gains and losses from asset values expressed in dollars of constant purchasing power for the year in which the taxes were to be paid. This could be done by multiplying the taxpayer's cost basis by the ratio of the general price index in the year of sale to the price index in the year of purchase ($10,000 times 1.5 in this case). Thus the investor would have an adjusted gain of $2,000 if he sold his asset for $17,000 and an adjusted loss of $1,000 if he sold it for $14,000. Similar price-level adjustments are not required for wages and salaries because under the current payment system the taxes are calculated and paid at about the same price level at which the income itself was earned and received. On the other hand, as discussed in chapter 2, annual adjustments in tax bracket boundaries, exemption levels, and deduction limits may be desirable for all kinds of income.

There is no doubt that indexing asset values for tax purposes would raise difficult practical problems and add considerable complexity to the tax law. In the first place, arriving at an appropriate general price index would not be easy. Second, taxpayers with assets fixed in money terms (deposits, bonds, mortgages, and so forth) would be entitled to capital loss deductions as prices increased, and this could either result in large revenue losses or require substantially higher tax rates to protect the revenue potential of the income tax. Third, persons with debt, who gain by inflation, would be required to pay tax on these gains and this would be strongly resisted. Fourth, although no one need worry about most taxpayers' acceptance of the procedure during inflation, their response during periods of falling price levels, when nominal losses would be converted into real gains, might be less than enthusiastic. Purchase of an asset for $10,000 and subsequent sale for $8,000 would produce a real capital gain of $3,000 if prices had fallen by 50 percent over the interval. Generally falling prices may seem too remote a possibility to merit consideration, but improvements in the productivity of business machines and equipment do produce reductions in the "real" price of those assets and advocates of replacement-cost depreciation might find this distinctly unwelcome. Finally, an adjustment for the price level would have to be offset by the benefits to be gained from postponing tax until realization.

Clearly, the best solution is to stabilize the general price level sufficiently to preclude any need for indexing. If this is not done, some form of indexing may be preferable to the simpler but less equitable alternatives that are likely to be offered in its stead.

Declining Inclusion Proportions

It is often proposed that, in the absence of indexing, the present method of taxing 50 percent of long-term capital gains should be replaced with one that would make the taxable portion smaller as the holding period increased. Proponents stress both the need to adjust more and more for inflation as holding periods lengthen and the inequity of taxing long-accrued and large gains all in one year at steeply progressive rates. Opponents note that no declining inclusion scale is capable of adjusting even approximately for different rates of inflation (to say nothing of periods of falling price levels) and that an explicit averaging scheme for long-term capital gains as well as for other income is already available to handle the bunching problem. The strongest criticism of the proposal is that the tax postponement benefits inherent in taxation on a realization basis increase with the length of the holding period and therefore justify a rising, rather than a declining, set of inclusion proportions.

Estimating the revenue losses that would be generated by reducing the inclusion percentage for long-term capital gains is difficult because of uncertainty about how much additional trading in capital assets might result. If no additional trading were stimulated, a reduction in the inclusion percentage from 50 percent to 25 percent would reduce 1976 revenues by $2.3 billion (table 3-1). The revenue loss, however, would be less if capital asset transfers were stimulated by the tax reduction.

Full Taxation of Capital Gains

Treating capital gains like other types of income by including them in taxable income in full has long been a goal of tax reformers. If tax

equity is to be improved and lock-in distortions avoided, full taxation must be accompanied, at a minimum, by a provision requiring
constructive realizations on gifts, bequests, and donations, by more
generous (or complete) loss offsets, and by suitable inflation (or
deflation) adjustments.[5] The tax law would be simplified by removing the distinction between short-term and long-term gains, but this
would be a minor accomplishment compared to eliminating the need
for the massive tangle of rules and regulations designed to prevent
taxpayers from converting ordinary income into preferentially taxed
capital gains. Some of these conversion schemes are discussed later.

Full taxation of capital gains on a realization basis, to be sure,
might unduly discourage the sales of capital assets and thus reduce
the fluidity of private capital markets. Although there is no presumption that it would, particularly if enacted with the accompanying features noted above, the contingency is worth serious consideration.
The risk could be reduced by a general lowering of the top marginal
tax rates on all types of income. Full taxation of realized capital gains
would raise revenues by $6.2 billion a year at 1976 levels, and the
addition of constructive realization would increase the revenue gain
to $11.1 billion (table 3-1). Both changes would permit substantial
reductions in the effective tax rates of persons with incomes of
$50,000 or more.

State and Local Government Bond Interest

Since 1913 interest from state and local government bonds has
been exempt from federal income taxes, and corresponding exemptions are granted for interest on federal securities under state and
local income taxes. This is a "bending-over-backwards" way of pro-
tecting intergovernmental immunities guaranteed by the Constitu-
tion, designed to protect the states against discriminatory treatment
by the federal government. These guarantees mean only that neither
level of government can apply a higher income tax rate to interest
on the other level's bonds than to interest on other securities. Most
tax and constitutional lawyers agree that taxation of state-local bond
interest by the federal government would be constitutional.

5. The averaging provision now in the tax law would be sufficient to avoid any
substantial discrimination resulting from the bunching of long-held capital gains in
a single year.

Pros and Cons of the Provision under Present Law

Critics of the state-local bond interest exemption stress the obvious violations of tax equity, the induced distortions of economic activity and of portfolio investment, and the inefficient nature of the subsidy that the federal government thereby grants to state and local agencies. Because of the exemption persons with the same economic income bear widely differing federal tax burdens; as would be expected, individual ownership of state and local bonds (25 to 30 percent of the total) is highly concentrated in the upper income groups where the tax advantage is the greatest. In recent years, for example, 70 to 80 percent of the interest on state and local bonds received by households has gone to those with marginal tax rates of 50 percent or more. Most other state and local bonds are owned by commercial banks (45 to 50 percent of the total) and by non-life insurance companies (about 10 to 15 percent of the total), and the shares of these companies, like all corporate shares, are mainly held by high income groups,[6] which thus reap the tax benefits of bond interest exemption. The result is that these investors, who are especially well situated to take the portfolio risks on which economic change and growth depend, put their money into low-risk state-local securities, which would normally be a prime source of income for less wealthy groups. At the same time, resources are diverted from the private to the public sector of the economy, a result that wealthy conservatives would ordinarily deplore.

The other side of the tax benefit coin is an inefficient federal subsidy to state and local governments. If the federal income tax were a broad-based proportional levy, both the benefit and the inefficiency would be eliminated by the wide competition for tax-exempt issues that would then prevail. If the tax rate were 25 percent and the interest rate on taxable bonds of comparable quality were 10 percent, for example, state and local securities should be salable at an interest rate of 7.5 percent. In such a case the entire subsidy of 2.5 percent would benefit state-local borrowers, and private investors would receive no more disposable income from tax-exempts than they do from taxable bonds. For the same result to occur under a

---

6. Ownership data are published annually by the Federal Reserve System in its flow-of-funds accounts. See, for example, *Federal Reserve Bulletin*, vol. 60 (October 1974), p. A59.18, table 7.

progressive income tax, the market for state and local bonds would have to be confined entirely to investors in the top tax bracket, and the supply of such securities has long since exceeded that limit.

If the market could be cleared only by selling bonds to 30 percent tax-bracket investors, the state-local interest rate would be 7 percent, and for an investor in the 70 percent tax bracket that rate would provide a subsidy of 4 percent since his best after-tax yield on taxable securities is 3 percent, an increase in the net yield from the investment of 133 percent. The more inequitable the tax-exempt feature, in other words, the less efficient the federal subsidy to state and local governments. This efficiency may be measured by the ratio of the interest saved by local and state governments to the revenue cost of the exemption to the federal government, and although it varies with money market conditions, in recent years it appears to have been between 70 and 75 percent.

Whatever the excess cost to the federal government may be, state and local governments do benefit from the tax exemption; for them it is an open-ended, no-strings-attached subsidy that would be difficult to replace. As a result, they are vigorous in its defense and are backed by those who fear that elimination of the exemption would drive state and local borrowing costs to unacceptably high levels, unduly impair these governments' ability to meet high-priority social needs, and, by increasing their budgetary expenditures, raise state and local taxes that already impose much heavier burdens on the lower and middle income classes than do federal taxes.

The interest exemption issue is further complicated by the problem of windfall gains and losses that would be generated by any tax reforms in this area. If the interest on all outstanding state and local securities were made taxable, present holders would suffer substantial capital losses. Since they have already borne an indirect tax burden in the form of a lower before-tax interest rate than they could otherwise have obtained on their investments, they would have legitimate grounds for complaint. On the other hand, if interest on only new issues of state and local bonds were made taxable, existing bonds would become more attractive and owners of long-term issues would enjoy capital gains that would gradually diminish as maturity dates came closer. Again, the present capital gains tax is an imperfect vehicle for the effective public recapture of such windfalls.

Replacement of the Tax Exemption
by a Federal Interest Subsidy

The windfalls require due consideration, but they are a necessary result of any policy change and are not the cause of the lack of action on tax-exempt bond interest. That has resulted from the interest groups that are sharply opposed to change. But there are signs of impending change. The most important one is an increasing disenchantment with the tax-exempt feature on the part of the state and local officials themselves. Their bonds have little appeal to lightly taxed investors, including such important sources of investment money as pension funds, mutual savings banks, savings and loan associations, colleges and universities, and life insurance companies. Experts anticipate that commercial banks will absorb a smaller portion of new state and local bond issues than in the past. Moreover, recent heavy reliance on monetary policy to stabilize the economy has subjected state and local governments to sharp and distressing swings in the demand for their bond offerings, as commercial banks have reacted to alternating periods of tight and easy money.

The key to the whole issue appears to be a broadly acceptable replacement for the tax-exempt interest subsidy. There has been no lack of candidates. Some experts have proposed a federally sponsored Urban Development Bank that would sell its own (taxable) securities in the open market and relend the proceeds to state and local governments at subsidized interest rates; some have suggested a direct federal subsidy for all state and local capital expenditures, regardless of whether they were financed by borrowing; still others support a federal subsidy to tax-exempt investors who purchase state and local securities. The chief difficulty with the first two proposals is the risk of federal controls and interference with state and local choice, now completely absent from the subsidized bond market. The third proposal avoids this difficulty, but it deals with only part of the now excluded market for state-local securities.

The most promising candidate for reform seems to be a direct federal subsidy payable on all taxable state and local bonds issued, with those governments remaining free to issue tax-exempts. With more taxable government bonds in the market, federal interest rates would be somewhat higher. At the same time, federal income tax receipts would be higher, and most of the increased revenue would come from the upper income groups. Investors would also find interest returns on whatever tax-exempt securities continued to be issued significantly reduced, and the tax-exemption subsidy would be correspondingly more efficient. Owners of tax-exempt securities issued before announcement of the subsidy plan, on the other hand, would enjoy capital gains.

Quantitative estimation of all of these effects requires the use of relatively large-scale econometric models and has only recently been feasible. It is estimated, for example, that a 40 percent taxable state-local bond subsidy would reduce interest rates on tax-exempts by more than half a percentage point, increase rates on taxable government bonds by a quarter of a percentage point, induce state and local governments to convert about one-eighth of their total bond issues to taxable form, and impose net costs on the Treasury that would increase gradually from only $50 million in the first year to a maximum of about $650 million. Holders of existing tax-exempt securities would enjoy capital gains of nearly $5 billion, but the prospect of reduced interest earnings on all new state and local bond issues would be equivalent to a current wealth loss of over $25 billion. Higher subsidy rates would increase all of these estimates, the biggest change coming at the point when commercial banks no longer found tax-exempts an attractive investment (presumably at a subsidy rate equal to the current corporation tax rate of 48 percent). A 50 percent subsidy, for example, would convert nearly 80 percent of the state-local bond market into taxable form but would raise net annual Treasury costs to an eventual maximum of nearly $2 billion.

A significant improvement in the equity and efficiency of the federal tax exemption subsidy to state and local governments does, then, appear to be a feasible policy option. Its potential distributional importance may be judged from table 3-2, which shows that almost $5 billion of federal tax revenues could be raised in 1976, mainly from the highest income classes, by making the interest on all outstanding state and local bond issues fully taxable. Unrealistic as that particular prospect may be, the figures do show the longer-run implications of more gradual policies designed with the same end in view.

Table 3-2. Revenue Effects of Taxing Interest on State and Local Government Bonds, by Adjusted Gross Income Class, 1976

Income classes in thousands of dollars

Revenue change and adjusted gross income class[a]	*Individuals*	*Corporations*	*Total*
Revenue change (millions of dollars)	1,300	3,600	4,900
Percentage distribution of revenue change			
0–3	*	1.6	1.2
3–5	0.5	4.2	3.2
5–10	0.5	8.6	6.4
10–15	0.8	8.6	6.6
15–20	1.3	8.8	6.8
20–25	1.4	5.4	4.3
25–50	13.3	19.7	18.0
50–100	41.7	18.7	24.8
100–200	34.7	10.5	16.9
200–500	5.3	7.1	6.6
500–1,000	0.2	2.7	2.0
1,000 and over	0.1	3.2	2.4
All classes[b]	100.0	100.0	100.0
Percentage change in tax liabilities			
0–3	0.9	138.6[c]	139.4[c]
3–5	0.6	13.1	13.7
5–10	0.1	2.8	2.9
10–15	0.1	1.6	1.6
15–20	0.1	1.3	1.4
20–25	0.1	1.0	1.2
25–50	0.6	2.3	2.9
50–100	3.6	4.4	8.0
100–200	6.0	5.0	11.0
200–500	2.0	7.3	9.3
500–1,000	0.2	9.8	10.1
1,000 and over	0.1	10.4	10.5
All classes[b]	1.0	2.7	3.7

Source: Brookings 1972 tax file, projected to 1976. Figures are rounded.
* Less than 0.05 percent.
a. Assumes corporation tax is borne by individuals in proportion to their dividend income.
b. Includes negative incomes not shown separately.
c. Percent increase in tax is unusually high because many persons with large incomes have tax shelters that reduce their adjusted gross income to less than $3,000 and pay virtually no individual income tax.

Investment Incentives: Accelerated
Depreciation and Tax Credits

Prominent among the economic priority issues of recent years has
been the extent to which governments should attempt to raise the
level of business investment or change its composition. Widespread
support for such action has drawn both tax specialists and econo-
metricians into a prolonged evaluation of alternative investment
tax incentives. In this country these have taken the form of accelerated depreciation (initiated in 1954 and extended in 1971)
and an investment tax credit (enacted in 1962, suspended in 1966–
67, repealed in 1969, reinstated in 1971, and raised in 1975). It
would be hard to find two more contrasting forms of investment tax
subsidy. Whereas accelerated depreciation is widely misunderstood,
well hidden from the general view, difficult to measure accurately,
and ambiguous in its impact on business profits, the investment tax
credit can be simple in structure, highly visible, readily measurable,
and less distorting in its effect on profits. The amount of the credit
can readily be varied as a means of stabilizing short-run fluctuations
in business investments; the tax rules governing depreciation patterns are, and should be, changed only rarely. It is these distinctive
qualities that make each tax measure an attractive subsidy from
some points of view but unattractive from others.

Part of the cost of earning income from the ownership of durable
assets that wear out gradually in use is the original investment made
in producing or purchasing those assets. These fixed costs must be
spread over the entire useful life of the assets and deducted from
gross income to reveal the true net gain, or economic income, being
received during any specific part of the total period of use. It is the
function of depreciation accounting to make these allocations. If all
used business plant and equipment could be sold on well-organized
competitive markets and if the general price level were stable, depreciation deductions could be derived directly from the observed
decline in market values of traded assets of the appropriate kind.
The lack of such markets requires the use of standardized depreciation patterns designed to reproduce as closely as possible the true
rate of economic depreciation on particular business assets. Exactly
what form these different patterns should take is still a highly contro-

versial question, particularly since they must take account not only of ordinary wear and tear but also of hard-to-predict technological and economic obsolescence. Finally, any failure to contain future inflationary forces would stimulate interest both in replacement-cost depreciation[7] and, more fundamentally, in the adjustment, or indexing, of all money values reported in business accounts for price level changes.

Useful Lives for Assets

The first requirement of depreciation accounting is an estimate of the expected useful life of all depreciable assets. While the Treasury has provided specific guidelines for some time, a major innovation was made in 1962, when "class lives" were adopted for broad groups of assets to simplify tax administration. As an incentive to modernization, these guideline lives were made shorter than those for about 70 percent of the assets in actual use in the group to enable businessmen, on the average, to recover full cost before the assets have to be retired from service. It was recognized that the use of such broad averages would result in excessively long or short depreciation periods in exceptional cases, and a means of relating tax depreciation to actual replacement practice—called "the reserve ratio test"—was provided for this purpose.[8] In view of the generous nature of the average guideline lives in the first place, the reserve ratio test was not likely to be popular with businessmen, and in 1971 its use to identify taxpayers who should use above-average service lives for their assets was discontinued. At the same time, guideline lives were changed from a single average for each class of asset to an "asset depreciation range system" that permitted taxpayers to select any service life for machinery and equipment within 20 percent (above or below) of the 1962 guideline averages. In effect, then, the 1971 revisions authorized

7. As the name suggests, under replacement-cost depreciation deductions over the useful life of an asset would be based not on the money originally spent to purchase the asset (as is done under traditional methods of depreciation accounting) but rather on the cost of replacing it with an identical asset at current price levels.

8. The reserve ratio is the ratio of the depreciation actually taken on a group of assets to their original cost. Benchmark values of the ratios, computed on the assumption that assets actually last for their exact tax service lives, were used by the Treasury to identify both taxpayers who replaced their assets frequently (and had a higher than normal reserve ratio) and were thus entitled to use even shorter tax service lives and taxpayers who used their assets for longer periods (and had a lower than normal reserve ratio) and should thus be required to use longer tax lives.

a 20 percent reduction in service lives for any businessman wishing to write off his depreciable asset investments more rapidly. The cost of this range system is estimated to be $1.7 billion at 1976 income and investment levels.

Another recent development, whose potential is still to be tested, is the revival of a fast write-off option, used earlier for defense and war facilities, to be applied to specific assets for which Congress discerns a high social need. The Tax Reform Act of 1969 authorized five-year, straight-line amortization for certain pollution control facilities, coal mine safety equipment, railroad rolling stock, and rehabilitation expenditures for low-income housing. The Revenue Act of 1971 did the same for employer-provided child care and on-the-job training facilities. These special allowances, which cost about $200 million a year, were continued for another year in 1974.

Depreciation Rate

The second requirement of depreciation accounting is a set of rules for the allocation of investment costs to each of the years of the asset's useful life. Traditionally this has been done by the "straight-line" method, which spreads the deductions uniformly—that is, allocating to each year one-fifth of the cost of a five-year asset, one-tenth of the cost of a ten-year asset, and so on. In 1954 two accelerated methods of allocation, known as "double declining-balance" and "sum-of-the-years-digits," were authorized.[9] The differences between these three methods are illustrated in table 3-3 for a $1,000 asset with a service life of ten years. Whereas with straight-line depreciation half the original cost of the asset is written off in the first five years, two-thirds is written off under the double declining-balance method and 73 percent under the sum-of-the-years-digits method. A convenient way of comparing the tax value of the three methods is shown in the last line of the table. For a corporation subject to a tax

9. Under the double declining-balance method, twice the straight-line rate of depreciation (that is, 20 percent for a ten-year asset) is applied to the undepreciated balance each year, with an option to shift to straight-line depreciation whenever more favorable to the taxpayer (in the seventh year for a ten-year asset). Under the sum-of-the-years-digits method, the depreciation rate for each year is the ratio of the number of years of remaining life to the sum of the years in the useful life $(55 = 10+9+8+\ldots+2+1)$, so that 10/55 of the cost is written off in the first year, 9/55 of the cost is written off in the second year, and so on until the last 1/55 is deducted in the tenth year.

Table 3-3. Comparison of Three Methods of Depreciation for a $1,000 Asset with Ten Years of Useful Life

Dollars

	Depreciation		
Year	Straight-line	Double declining-balance[a]	Sum-of-the-years-digits[b]
1	100	200	182
2	100	160	164
3	100	128	145
4	100	102	127
5	100	82	109
6	100	66	91
7	100	65.5	73
8	100	65.5	55
9	100	65.5	36
10	100	65.5	18
Total	1,000	1,000	1,000
Present value at 8 percent			
Depreciation	671	733	748
Tax value of depreciation allowances at tax rate of 48 percent	322	352	359

a. Twice the straight-line rate of depreciation is applied to the undepreciated balance each year, with an option to shift to straight-line depreciation whenever more favorable to the taxpayer.

b. The depreciation rate for each year is the ratio of the number of years of remaining life to the sum of the years in the useful life.

rate of 48 percent and using an after-tax rate of return of 8 percent to evaluate future earning possibilities, the present value of all future tax savings from sum-of-the-years-digits depreciation would be $359, but from straight-line depreciation it would be only $322, a difference that is 3.7 percent of the original cost of the asset.

There has been considerable confusion about the exact meaning of accelerated depreciation. Some view it as any deduction pattern that is more rapid than straight-line depreciation, but there is nothing special about the latter other than its long-standing use. The appropriate standard is economic depreciation, equal to the decline in the market value of the depreciable asset during the period under consideration, because it has the distinctive quality of producing measures of true economic income, the ideal base for equitable income taxation. Another way of putting it is that use of economic depreciation keeps the book value of a depreciable asset (original cost minus depreciation deductions) always equal to its market value. All other depreciation patterns produce capital gains or losses when a depreciable asset is sold before the end of its economic life.

With economic depreciation as the accepted standard it may be concluded that less rapid (decelerated) depreciation patterns impose heavier tax burdens on income from depreciable assets than on other kinds of income and in the process discourage new business investment. More rapid (accelerated) patterns impose light tax burdens and thereby stimulate new investment. Whether any specific pattern is accelerated or decelerated in this sense is an important tax policy question that requires considerable empirical analysis to answer. It now appears, for example, that straight-line depreciation is too generous for buildings but not generous enough for many kinds of business equipment.

The tax value of accelerated depreciation comes mainly from the postponement of tax liability, though in some cases there are additional gains from converting ordinary income, taxable at regular rates, into capital gains, taxable at lower rates. Tax postponement is equivalent to an unsecured, interest-free loan of indefinite maturity made by the Treasury to the taxpayer. Its economic value is highly variable, depending on the circumstances, but is frequently substantial. In general, it is larger when interest rates are high, when outside capital is difficult to obtain, when long-lived assets are purchased, and when the recipient firm is growing rapidly. Indeed, simply by growing at a constant rate a firm can indefinitely keep its annual tax liability under accelerated depreciation below that which would be due if it used economic depreciation.

The capital gains conversion feature of accelerated depreciation may be illustrated by supposing that the $1,000 asset shown in table 3-3 is worth $900 at the end of three years of service life and is then sold by the owner. The book value at that time under double declining-balance depreciation would be $512, and a long-term capital gain of $388 would consequently be realized. This gain has been created entirely by the excess depreciation taken ($488 less $100 equals $388) and deducted from income subject to full tax rates. Its tax value to a corporation is therefore $186 (0.48 times $388), and it would be exactly recouped only if the subsequent capital gain were taxed at the same tax rate (that is, as ordinary income). Under present recapture provisions this would indeed be the case for machinery and equipment, but for real property, where the recapture is confined to the excess of deductions taken over straight-line depreciation, only $188 ($488 less $300) of the capital gain would be taxed as ordinary income and the rest at the corporate long-term capital gains rate of 30 percent. Moreover, in the case of rental property this recapture provision is phased out for longer holding periods.[10]

Another feature of accelerated depreciation is its impact on reported profits. Since it shows these as lower than they would be under economic depreciation, corporate managers are faced with a dilemma. If they base their financial reports on economic depreciation in order to give an accurate picture of the corporation's profitability, they automatically publicize the subsidy features built into tax depreciation allowances and may thereby weaken the case for their continuation. If, on the other hand, they base their financial reports on accelerated tax depreciation, they automatically underreport the level of their profits (as long as the corporation is growing) and risk misleading investors and others. Like other hidden subsidies, in other words, accelerated tax depreciation could misdirect, as well as stimulate, business investments. However, in recent years corporations have not used tax depreciation for purposes of public accounting, so the distortion is not great.

The Investment Credit

These considerations provide a strong argument for setting tax depreciation as close to economic depreciation as possible and for providing whatever investment incentives or disincentives are deemed desirable by the use of separate policy instruments. The simplest and broadest possibility would be a federal subsidy providing for the payment of a stated percentage of all new investment expenditures to the business firms making them. The subsidy rate for this open-ended government grant could normally be set at the level thought desirable for growth policy purposes and then varied around that level (including negative as well as positive rates) for short-run stabilization purposes. Unlike the more familiar tax subsidy approach, such a program would cover all businesses, whether making taxable profits

10. There is full recapture if the property is held for one hundred months; thereafter, the recapture percentage decreases 1 percent for each month until the property has been held for more than sixteen years and eight months, or two hundred months, when there is no recapture.

or not, and would be subject to the more stringent budgetary reviews applied to government expenditures. Advocates of minimal government interference in economic affairs are likely to prefer the visibility of such an expenditure subsidy program, while some supporters of a strong sustained commitment to high economic growth value the lower exposure of tax subsidies to budgetary pressures.

First adopted in 1962, the investment credit is a major innovation in federal tax policy. Under it a business firm may deduct, as a credit against its federal income tax liability, a specified fraction of its new investment expenditures for tangible personal property with a service life of seven years or more. From 1971 to 1974 the credit rates were 7 percent for business generally and 4 percent for public utilities, but in 1975 both rates were increased to 10 percent as an anti-recessionary stimulus to investments made in 1975 and 1976.[11] One-third of the full credit is allowed on three-to-five-year assets and two-thirds on five-to-seven-year assets, a feature that adjusts for the tendency of all investment credits to favor short-lived over long-lived assets. While full deduction is allowed against the first $25,000 of tax liability, it is normally restricted to 50 percent of the remainder. The Tax Reduction Act of 1975, however, eliminated the 50 percent restriction for public utilities for 1975 and 1976 and provided for its gradual reinstatement, beginning at 90 percent in 1977 and declining to the normal 50 percent in 1981 and thereafter.

Unused investment credits may be carried back for three years and forward for seven. For many businesses these constraints have created a stock of unused credits ($1.3 billion in 1970) whose value is difficult to assess because of uncertainty about when and to what extent they will be deductible against future tax liabilities. The proper accounting treatment of currently deducted credits is also vague. Should they be allowed to reduce current after-tax profits by their full amount or should they be capitalized and deducted gradually over the service life of the asset on whose purchase they were earned? Accounting for the investment credit, in short, is as subject to ambiguities as accounting for accelerated depreciation. The one difference is that with the latter the difficulties apply to both before-tax and after-tax profits; with the investment tax credit they apply only to

11. An additional 1 percent credit is allowed in these two years if the employer establishes an employee stock ownership plan and uses that amount to purchase the firm's securities for the plan.

after-tax earnings. Finally, the present version of the investment credit does not reduce the amount of depreciation that firms may take on their qualified investments. But under a subsidy, tax depreciation would presumably be based on each firm's actual investment expenditures, which would equal the net-of-subsidy cost of the assets acquired. A similar reduction-of-depreciation-basis rule applied to the 1962 version of the investment credit but was eliminated in 1964. At 1976 income and investment levels the cost of the liberalized investment credit is estimated to be $6.2 billion.

Alternative Revisions

Tax policy options for business investment and economic growth may be grouped into three broad sets, here arranged in descending order of interference with current tax law.

1. *A minimum government support approach.* This would mean making a judgment that both private investment levels and economic growth rates are best left to the determination of the free market. The present investment tax credit would accordingly be eliminated, tax service lives for depreciable assets would be lengthened so as to move them as close to actual economic lifetimes as possible, and tax depreciation patterns would be based on economic depreciation. As with all subsidies closely related to profit income, the vertical distribution of tax increases resulting from their elimination would be highly progressive. A major deterrent to any quick adoption of the minimum government support program is the wide disparity between existing market structures and the optimal ones hypothesized by laissez-faire economists. It may be those very imperfections, including some imposed by other parts of the tax system, that create the real need for government investment incentives. If so, complete elimination of the incentives may come only in the last phases of a coordinated attack on all major free market distortions.

2. *A steady growth priority approach.* If economic growth is accorded a high social priority, for whatever reasons, and if the economic efficiencies associated with widespread use of economic depreciation accounting are to be realized, the principal public instrument would be a revised investment tax credit system. In addition to eliminating accelerated depreciation, changes from present law would include:

—some increase in the investment tax credit rate structure to counteract the investment deterrent effects of eliminating accelerated depreciation;

—institution of a range of investment tax credit rates within which changes would be made for short-run stabilization purposes;

—an easing, or elimination, of the present 50 percent tax liability constraint for individual firms; or

—addition of a cash payment system for all investment tax credits in excess of the taxpayer's current income tax liability and elimination of the present carry-over rules. This change would convert the support system into a set of open-ended, matching government grants administered through the federal income tax system.

3. *A steady-as-you-go approach.* If existing business investment incentives are regarded as about adequate so that the costs of any major change are likely to outweigh the potential benefits, the appropriate tax policy prescription is one, in Senator Russell B. Long's words, of "tightening up the loose ends and loosening up the tight ends." Included among the loose ends might be the 1971 asset depreciation range system and the 1969–71 special five-year amortization options, and included in the tight ends might be the 50 percent tax liability constraint on deductible investment tax credits. For any desired level of government stimulus of business investment this third approach would call for a lower investment tax credit than would the second, and the permissible range of variation for short-run stabilization purposes could consequently extend into negative values (a tax surcharge on business investment during periods of high inflation).

Whatever the specific approach taken, the basic social priorities are more or less income redistribution in the short run, higher or lower rates of economic growth in the long run, and more or less government intervention in the allocation of resources to different industries and in the determination of the economic lives of durable business assets. Empirical measurement of the economic inefficiencies involved in all of these choices is still in a rudimentary stage, but its accelerating development does promise better policy guidance in the future.

Investment Incentives: Mineral Industry Subsidies

Investment incentives of a different kind are provided for the oil, gas, and other mineral industries by generous expensing rules for certain capital costs and by percentage depletion allowances that have been part of federal tax law for many years but were eliminated in 1975 for the major oil companies. Presumably the chief social purpose of these subsidies is to encourage the development of extra mineral capacity which the United States might need in some future national emergency. National security, however, is not the only justification that has been advanced in favor of mineral subsidies.

Rationale for Mineral Tax Subsidies

One argument, with considerable superficial appeal, is that mineral exploration and development, and particularly oil and gas operations, are subject to excessive economic risks that justify special tax treatment. Neither part of this proposition is firmly established. Every business undertaking is subject to risks, and no objective identification of especially high risk areas can be said to exist. While few wildcat oil wells may turn out to be productive, the ratio of successful to unsuccessful wells has been remarkably stable (at one to nine), permitting drillers of large numbers of exploratory wells to predict quite accurately the number of successes they are likely to have. More fundamentally, government subsidization of high risk enterprises would be called for only if private markets adjusted insufficiently to give investors higher average rates of return in those industries. Furthermore, even if some government subsidy was thought advisable, tax incentives would not necessarily be the most efficient means of achieving the result desired. The "excessive risk" case for mineral tax incentives, then, is a complex one whose specific dimensions have not yet gone much beyond the assertion stage.

But the ideal income tax treatment of risky enterprises does have some special features. Suppose that one wildcat well in ten is productive and that for the average enterprise, as would be true under equilibrium conditions, the discovery value of a successful well is ten times the direct costs of bringing it into production. Annual exploration and development costs, which would tend to equal the current market value of newly discovered productive wells during the year, would normally be capitalized and deducted from gross income as a depletion allowance over the lifetime of the wells. For more fortunate companies, discovery values would tend to exceed exploration costs, and these enterprises would have the choice of operating the successful wells themselves and receiving the extra gain as ordinary income from production or of selling the properties and receiving it as capital gains. Any favorable tax treatment of the latter kind of income would bias that choice toward immediate sale. On the other hand, exploration costs for less successful companies would be greater than discovery values, and under an ideal economic income tax these losses would be reimbursed as incurred at the standard rate of income tax. In other words, a proportional income tax with full offsets for losses against other income would reimburse this year's losses at the same rate as this year's gains were being taxed, and such a tax would have the important feature of not changing the rate of reward for risk taking.

The present corporation income tax falls short of the ideal because of the limitations it places on loss offsets. While the three-year carry-back for net operating losses is equivalent to an immediate cash rebate for generally profitable companies, for others it is of limited value, and the five-year carry-forward on which they must rely instead is worth less to them than immediate reimbursement. Current law also places various restrictions on the carry-over of net losses from one corporation to another, and because of its progressive rate structure the individual income tax may tax gains at a higher average rate than it reimburses losses. For investors generally, then, federal income tax law tends to lower the after-tax rate of return to risk-taking.

For the oil and gas industries, on the other hand, current tax law provides one important advantage: permission to write off intangible drilling and development costs on a current basis rather than capitalizing them and deducting them gradually over the lifetime of the producing wells. A special percentage depletion deduction was also allowed for many years, first at 27.5 percent of gross receipts and later at 22 percent, but this was eliminated in 1975 for the major oil companies and gradually reduced for the others over the following nine years.[12] Similar expensing privileges and lower-rate depletion

12. The percentage depletion allowance will be phased down for small producers of oil and gas from 22 percent in 1975–80, to 20 percent in 1981, 18 percent in 1982, 16 percent in 1983, and 15 percent in 1984 and thereafter. Small producers are defined as those producing 2,000 barrels of oil a day in 1975, with reductions of 200 barrels a day in succeeding years until 1980, when the limit will be 1,000 barrels a day. For natural gas, the limit is 12 million cubic feet a day in 1975, which will be phased down to 6 million cubic feet a day in 1980 and thereafter. Small producers constitute all but a few of all producers.

allowances still apply to other mineral producers. Treasury estimates place the revenue gain from the 1975 limitation on percentage depletion at $1.6 billion in that year. As table 3-4 indicates, complete elimination of percentage depletion and its replacement with cost depletion, together with compulsory capitalization of intangible drilling and development costs, would raise federal tax revenues in 1976 by another $3.2 billion. Most of the increases would affect individuals with adjusted gross incomes above $25,000 a year.

Proponents of mineral tax subsidies argue that they are a necessary corrective device for other distortions firmly embedded in the tax law. Such arguments have a nightmare quality, with one tax bias justifying another, which in turn justifies several others, which then justify still others in an endless escalation with no real rationale. There has been in any case an extended technical debate over whether the oil and gas tax provisions have distorted the allocation of resources by moving investment into those industries away from the higher economic returns obtainable elsewhere, with consequent heavy efficiency losses for the economy, or whether the provisions simply offset the allocative distortions imposed by a corporation income tax that is fully shifted forward to consumers and that consequently discriminates against capital-intensive industries such as oil and gas. Because of present uncertainty about the incidence and other economic effects of the corporate profits tax, these arguments are not easy to evaluate, but economists who have examined the issue generally believe that on balance the allocation of resources is significantly distorted by the subsidies.

If mineral tax subsidies do change the allocation of resources from what it would be in a no-tax or completely neutral-tax economy, the remaining questions are whether such change is consistent with the requirements of national security, whether that particular priority justifies the tax costs of the present subsidies, and whether the same goals could not be achieved more efficiently by using other policy instruments. The first two of these questions are inherently difficult, if not impossible, to answer, and quantitative answers to the third question have just begun to appear. A major technical analysis, prepared for the Treasury Department as part of its 1969 tax reform studies, concluded that percentage depletion is a relatively inefficient method of raising oil and gas reserves. Partly this is because, according to the analysis, less than 60 percent of the subsidy

Table 3-4. Revenue Effects of Revisions of Tax Provisions Applying to Oil, Gas, and Other Minerals, by Adjusted Gross Income Class, 1976

Income classes in thousands of dollars

Revenue change and adjusted gross income class	Eliminate percentage depletion			Require capitalization of intangible drilling and development expenses		
	Individuals	Corporations[a]	Total	Individuals	Corporations[a]	Total
Revenue change (millions of dollars)	800	800	1,600	150	1,500	1,650
	Percentage distribution of revenue change					
0–3	0.1	1.6	0.9	0.1	1.6	1.5
3–5	*	4.2	2.1	*	4.2	3.8
5–10	0.4	8.6	4.5	0.4	8.6	7.8
10–15	0.1	8.6	4.4	0.1	8.6	7.8
15–20	0.4	8.8	4.6	0.4	8.8	8.1
20–25	*	5.4	2.7	*	5.4	4.9
25–50	10.1	19.7	14.9	11.4	19.7	18.9
50–100	9.1	18.7	13.9	9.8	18.7	17.9
100–200	29.6	10.5	20.1	27.4	10.5	12.1
200–500	24.3	7.1	15.7	21.8	7.1	8.4
500–1,000	10.6	2.7	6.6	9.5	2.7	3.3
1,000 and over	13.1	3.2	8.1	11.6	3.2	4.0
All classes[b]	100.0	100.0	100.0	100.0	100.0	100.0
	Percentage change in tax liabilities					
0–3	1.3	30.8[c]	32.1[c]	0.4	57.7[c]	58.2[c]
3–5	*	2.9	2.9	*	5.5	5.5
5–10	*	0.6	0.7	*	1.2	1.2
10–15	*	0.3	0.4	*	0.6	0.6
15–20	*	0.3	0.3	*	0.6	0.6
20–25	*	0.2	0.2	*	0.4	0.4
25–50	0.3	0.5	0.8	0.1	1.0	1.0
50–100	0.5	1.0	1.5	0.1	1.8	1.9
100–200	3.1	1.1	4.2	0.5	2.1	2.6
200–500	5.6	1.6	7.2	0.9	3.0	4.0
500–1,000	8.7	2.2	10.9	1.5	4.1	5.6
1,000 and over	9.4	2.3	11.7	1.6	4.3	5.9
All classes[b]	0.6	0.6	1.2	0.1	1.1	1.2

Source: Brookings 1972 tax file, projected to 1976. Figures are rounded.
* Less than 0.05 percent.
a. Assumes corporation tax is borne by individuals in proportion to their dividend income.
b. Includes negative incomes not shown separately.
c. Percent increase in tax is unusually high because many persons with large incomes have tax shelters that reduce their adjusted gross income to less than $3,000 and pay virtually no individual income tax.

accrued to domestic operating interests (the remainder went either to foreign producers or to domestic nonoperating interests), and partly because the study's estimates showed the level of oil and gas reserves desired by business to be insensitive to price subsidies of the kind generated by percentage depletion. The option to expense intangibles, on the other hand, was found to be more efficient, although it too lacks incentive power when its benefits are shifted away from producers to either consumers (as lower prices) or leaseholders and landowners (as higher royalties and land values).

Alternative Revisions

Tax reformers have three main policy options in the treatment of the mineral industries. The first, begun in 1975, would eliminate percentage depletion for most or all mineral enterprises, which would then recover their capital costs by means of cost depletion. The heightened importance of cost depletion might then justify further study of realistic service lives for different kinds of mines and of optimal allocation patterns for depletion deductions over those lifetimes. A side effect worth watching would be the increased incentives for intercompany sales of proved oil and gas wells; in such sales the discovery profits are taxed as capital gains rather than ordinary income.

A second reform would eliminate existing expensing privileges for all capital costs of mineral enterprises and require recovery through cost depletion deductions. This would have a greater negative impact on oil and gas reserves than the elimination of percentage depletion, though the effects would be quite sensitive to the speed with which cost depletion deductions were allowed for tax purposes.

Removal of all tax subsidies for the mineral industries would direct public attention to the need for special defense mineral reserves and to the most efficient ways of achieving them. If fast tax write-offs of exploration and development costs for this purpose were regarded as superior to direct subsidies, it would then be appropriate to consider the third tax reform option, one that would expand present capital cost expensing privileges to cover all exploration and development expenses, both tangible and intangible, for minerals requiring special defense reserves that could not be provided more effectively by other means.

Tax Shelters

Tax shelters have been much in the public eye of late, sometimes basking in the warm glow of the favorable publicity created by promoters and successful practitioners, sometimes shivering in the cold, critical blasts emanating from tax reformers intent on eliminating them. They include a wide range of activities—most notably, rental real estate, oil wells, cattle feeding and breeding, orchards and vineyards, and machinery and equipment leasing—and also promise some rather spectacular net-of-tax rates of return. Thus a modest 2 percent before-tax rate of return on low-income rental housing rehabilitation can yield a 24 percent after-tax rate of return for an investor in the 50 percent tax bracket. Even more dramatically, a negative before-tax rate of return on leasing locomotives to a railroad can be converted into a positive 20 percent after-tax rate of return for the investor with a 70 percent tax bracket. But high rates of return to specific investors may indicate either exceptional risk-taking or the careful use of tax advantages. To keep tax reform measures from being counterproductive, it is imperative to distinguish between the two.

Elements of Tax Shelter Arrangements

Tax shelters combine three basic elements in varying degrees: tax deferral, heavy reliance on borrowing, and the capital gains tax advantage. Of these the most important for tax reformers is the postponement feature, which gives the projects in question their name. By investing in activities that involve immediate capital costs but little or no return until much later, the taxpayer can, by deducting those net costs, shelter the income from these activities as well as some of his other current income from tax burdens it would otherwise incur. If the economic income of a project is indeed negative, it deserves a negative tax burden, and instead of the government's reimbursing the investor in cash at the appropriate rate, an efficient alternative is to allow him to deduct his losses from any other current income he may have. In this way tax equity is preserved and risk-taking incentives protected. Quite the opposite results, however, when the negative income of a project is created by the use of accelerated depreciation or by the current expensing of capital costs.

Not only are large tax advantages then extended to a favored few, but investment funds are also misdirected into particular areas where the before-tax rate of return, which is the one that indicates the economic value to society of the activity in question, may be driven down to a ridiculously low level. In addition, valuable man-hours are expended on the promotion and sale of tax shelter investments to the rich.

Alternative Revisions

Although direct elimination of these tax abuses, because it subjects all capital costs to the economic depreciation rules discussed earlier and adopts full taxation of capital gains, is the preferable solution, the political and other difficulties of such a course have stimulated serious consideration of a number of second-best solutions. One possibility would be to limit the deduction of business losses to related kinds of business income—say, losses from a given housing project could be deducted only from current profits realized by the taxpayer on other housing investments—and to provide for the carry-over of losses that cannot be offset for similar use in later years. This would eliminate the sheltering of unrelated income from current tax burdens, but at the cost of discriminating against legitimate investments and discouraging diversification in investor portfolios. A better though more complex solution would be to divide business losses into two categories, artificial and economic, and to apply the restrictions just described only to the former.

A third approach would be to reduce the tax advantages of heavy borrowing by restricting capital cost expensing and accelerated depreciation privileges to the investor's own capital plus repayment of principal on his indebtedness. For instance, on a $5 million rental building purchased with the help of $4 million of borrowed funds, the deduction of any depreciation greater than economic depreciation could be restricted at first to the owner's $1 million equity, and later deductions beyond that amount would be allowed only on the portion of the loan that had been repaid. While this would work with taxpayers whose investments were concentrated in tax shelter projects, those with broader portfolios could avoid the restrictions simply by borrowing on the security of nonshelter assets and using the proceeds to acquire a 100 percent equity in some shelter project.

Finally, the capital gains tax advantage that results from capital cost expensing and accelerated depreciation could be eliminated by extending "recapture of income" features, initiated in 1962 and expanded in 1964 and 1969, to all projects involving tax deferral. Thus all gains that simply reflect the earlier deferral of ordinary income would be taxed as ordinary income and not as capital gains. The main areas not yet fully covered in this way include oil, rental housing, commercial buildings, and farm operations. Recapture provisions would also be improved by using economic rather than straight-line depreciation as the basis for the calculations.

The problem with second-best solutions is that they create new problems while solving old ones. They are often both complicated and crude, sacrificing tax simplicity merely to achieve partial reductions of tax advantages and in the process discriminating against some legitimate and valuable investment activities. For the tax reformer they pose a difficult dilemma. Should he push for their adoption because they are better than nothing, even though their enactment might delay or even preclude the best reforms, or should he put up with an imperfect tax system a little longer in the hope of achieving a better one later? The choice is not unlike that between consumption and saving in a highly uncertain world.

The revenue effect of such revisions could be substantial. Limiting the deduction of real estate losses to related income (with indefinite carry-overs to future years) would raise business taxes $700 million a year. Restricting deductions for depreciation and taxes to the taxpayer's own capital invested in the project would not raise a large amount of revenue, at least in the early years. Extending the recapture-of-income provisions for depreciation previously taken on real estate to investments not already covered would add $100 million of revenue annually. People with low income are not involved in these arrangements; the revenue gained from such revisions would come entirely from high income people and corporations.

Allocation of Personal Deductions

A second-best tax reform of broader scope, which in 1969 was accepted by the House Ways and Means Committee but rejected by the Senate Finance Committee, is the compulsory allocation of personal deductions into allowable and nonallowable categories in accordance with the division of the taxpayer's taxable and nontaxable income. Proponents argue that tax deductibility privileges should be extended only to the qualifying personal expenses that are actually financed by taxable income. Tax equity between those with taxable income only and those with both taxable and exempt income therefore requires some restriction on the deductions that the latter group can itemize. The few expenses that are specifically allocable to tax-exempt income sources, such as interest on debt incurred to purchase municipal bonds, should not be deductible at all. But most itemizable expenses cannot be specifically allocated to particular income sources, and for them the reasonable presumption is that they are financed proportionately from the taxpayer's taxable and nontaxable sources of income.

Implementation of the allocation of deductions proposal would require three major decisions.

1. *Above the line deductions.* Some itemized deductions represent amounts spent to earn fully taxable income and hence should be fully deductible in computing adjusted gross income. Items that should be moved above the adjusted gross income line for this reason, regardless of whether deductions are allocated between taxable and nontaxable sources, include occupational and professional expenses (union dues, subscriptions to professional journals, and so forth), and investment expenses that do not exceed taxable investment income. Other expenses, such as alimony and charitable contributions, are more debatable. Some argue that charitable gifts, being neither personal consumption nor personal saving, do not fall within the measure of ability to pay taxes and hence should be fully excluded from taxable income. Others, viewing income more broadly and charitable contributions as a deduction allowed because they promote socially meritorious activities, would subject those contributions to compulsory allocation unless the effects on giving proved excessively discouraging.

2. *Allocation formula.* All other personal deduction expenditures would then be allocated into deductible and nondeductible categories on the basis of the following formula:

$$\text{allowable personal deductions} = \text{total personal deduction expenditures} \times \frac{\text{adjusted gross income}}{\text{adjusted gross income} + \text{preference income}}.$$

Those with relatively unimportant amounts of preference income—

$10,000 has been suggested as a reasonable compromise at current price levels between equity and administrative considerations—could be exempted from the allocation provision entirely. In addition, a minimum amount of personal deductions—say, $2,000—could be allowed without allocation.

3. *Definition of preference income.* The most difficult decision would be determining which items should be included in preference income in the allocation formula. For some fully exempt income sources there would be little or no problem. Examples are the excluded half of long-term capital gains, the excess of percentage over economic cost depletion, and exempt income earned abroad. Inclusion of interest on state and local bonds, however, might require some compensating federal aid that could be better handled in one of the more direct ways discussed earlier. Unrealized appreciation on property given to charities poses a special problem—its full inclusion in preference income would frequently disallow part of the charitable contribution deduction and thereby convert part of the unrealized appreciation into nonpreference income. The correct inclusion portion could be calculated by the use of simultaneous-equations algebra, but a more direct reform, such as constructive realization of all capital gains accrued on property given to charities, seems preferable. The most troublesome items of all would be the various tax deferral privileges whose value to the taxpayer, being some unknown fraction of the income sheltered from current taxation, remains unknown until the end of the deferral period. Inclusion of such tax provisions as accelerated depreciation, capital cost expensing, and stock option gains would therefore require some compensating tax credit at the end of the investment period, and would complicate the tax law accordingly.

Because of these structural uncertainties, no single estimate of the revenue effects of the allocation proposal can give more than a rough indication of the magnitudes involved. One such estimate is given in table 3-5; it is based on the assumption that all itemized personal deductions over $2,000 a return are made subject to compulsory allocation, with state-local bond interest, as well as capital gains and other preference items, counted as income from which the deductible outlays are presumed to be paid. About two-thirds of the estimated 1976 tax increase of $1.9 billion would be borne by taxpayers with adjusted gross income above $25,000.

Table 3-5. Revenue Effects of Compulsory Allocation of Personal Deductions between Taxable and Nontaxable Income, by Adjusted Gross Income Class, 1976
Income classes in thousands of dollars

Revenue change and adjusted gross income class	Compulsory allocation of deductions[a]
Revenue change	
(millions of dollars)	1,900
Percentage distribution of revenue change	
0–3	*
3–5	*
5–10	2.5
10–15	8.1
15–20	12.3
20–25	10.5
25–50	19.9
50–100	14.7
100–200	11.9
200–500	7.7
500–1,000	3.9
1,000 and over	8.4
All classes[b]	100.0
Percentage change in tax liabilities	
0–3	*
3–5	*
5–10	0.4
10–15	0.8
15–20	1.0
20–25	1.1
25–50	1.3
50–100	1.9
100–200	3.1
200–500	4.3
500–1,000	7.8
1,000 and over	14.8
All classes[b]	1.5

Source: Brookings 1972 tax file, projected to 1976. Figures are rounded.
* Less than 0.05 percent.
a. All itemized personal deductions in excess of $2,000 allocated between adjusted gross income and nontaxable income (state-local bond interest, excluded capital gains, and other preference items subject to the minimum tax).
b. Includes negative incomes not shown separately.

Minimum Tax

Another second-best general tax reform measure is the minimum tax initiated by the Tax Reform Act of 1969. Stimulated by the dramatic revelation in early 1969 that, in 1967, 155 persons with adjusted gross income of over $200,000 and 21 with income of over $1 million paid no federal income taxes at all, Congress added to the tax law a feature that may become an important means of controlling excessive tax avoidance. For a selected list of tax preference income items, a minimum tax of 10 percent is levied on the amount by which they exceed (1) a $30,000 exemption, (2) the regular federal income tax liability of the year, and since 1970 (3) any unused tax liability deductions from any of the past seven years. By far the most important preference income item included in the minimum tax base, accounting for about 85 percent of the total for individuals, is the excluded half of long-term capital gains. Other items include excessive depreciation and depletion, excessive deductions by financial institutions to maintain reserves for losses on bad debts, and the capital gain element in stock options. Conspicuous by its absence is exempt interest on state and local bonds.

Because of its generous exemptions, low rate, and restricted coverage, the minimum tax is regarded by many as a weak and inadequate attack on tax privileges. It has also been a disappointing source of revenue to the Treasury. The number of no-tax-due returns with adjusted gross income above $200,000 declined from 300 in 1969 to 99 in 1972. However, although 1970 revenues were projected to be $285 million from individuals and $350 million from corporations, actual receipts were only $122 million and $218 million in 1970 and $169 million and $279 million in 1972.

Any proposal to strengthen or restructure the minimum tax raises three basic policy questions.

1. Should the tax be a supplementary or an alternative levy? The former type is appropriate if the goal is to levy a minimum tax on all preference income above some minimum absolute amount. On the other hand, if taxpayers with large regular tax liabilities are seen as deserving tax advantages more than those with small regular tax liabilities, an alternative tax, payable only if it exceeds the regular tax, is the appropriate form of minimum tax.

2. Should the rate structure be proportional or progressive? For a supplementary tax, one added to the individual's regular liability, a case can be made for either approach, although in both instances special care would be needed to preclude excessive total burdens on some taxpayers. But an alternative tax would presumably use a progressive rate structure for individuals and a proportional one for corporations. One possibility would be to apply the regular tax rates to some fraction of an expanded tax base composed of adjusted gross income augmented by specified tax preference income items and reduced by a more restricted list of deductions and exemptions than are now allowed in the computation of taxable income. If the fraction chosen were one-half, the effect would be to allow one dollar of taxable income to shelter as much as one dollar of preference income, with minimum tax becoming due on larger amounts of the latter.[13] In that sense the plan would be a generous one, and as long as the excluded portion of long-term capital gains did not exceed one-half, no additional tax would be imposed on them by this plan. Unless other significant preference items were added to the base, such a minimum tax would be largely window dressing.

3. What should the breadth of the minimum tax base be? While ideally the base should be made as broad as possible, two practical difficulties would arise. One would be created by the preference items, such as exempt state-local bond interest, charitable contributions, and nonbusiness state-local tax payments, that function as incentive or subsidy devices. The matter might be better handled by direct reform measures that preserved the desirable features while eliminating inequities and inefficiencies. Attempts to include them in the minimum tax base might simply prevent desirable tax revision.

The second difficulty would be created by tax deferral items, some of which are now included in the minimum tax base. Consider an investor in the 70 percent tax bracket who shelters $100 of current income from tax by deducting excess depreciation of that amount from his gross business income. If he were subject to a current mini-

13. With a 50 percent inclusion factor a taxpayer with $50,000 of taxable income and $50,000 of preference income would have exactly the same tax liability ($17,060 on a joint return in 1975) under either alternative since his minimum tax base would be one-half of $100,000. A taxpayer with $25,000 in taxable and $75,000 in preference income, however, would owe a regular tax of only $6,020 but a minimum tax of $17,060.

mum tax of $35 on that amount, and if some years hence when the property was sold that excess depreciation were subject to recapture rules, making the $100 gain taxable as ordinary income, he would then owe $70 in tax and have a total levy on the $100 preference income of $105. Confiscatory as this may look at first glance, it may in reality be too low a tax burden. By sheltering $100 from tax the investor gains the annual income he can earn by investing the post-poned tax amount. If he can invest at 10 percent, his annual net-of-tax income on the $70 postponed tax will be $2.10 ($7.00 minus 0.7 of $7.00), and the present value of this future income stream, discounted at his after-tax rate of return of 2.1 percent, is about $19 if he defers tax for ten years, $35 if he defers it for twenty years, and about $47 if he defers it for thirty years. The initial minimum tax liability of $35, in other words, would be the correct assessment for a holding period of twenty years; less should be collected for shorter periods and more for longer ones.

Two solutions have been suggested to the tax deferral problem. One would include deferral preferences in the minimum tax base at full value but allow for holding periods inconsistent with that treat-ment by means of a tax credit for shorter periods and an additional charge for longer ones. Compared with direct elimination of the tax deferral preferences, this approach would dispense rough justice in a complex fashion. A second solution would restrict the minimum tax to fully exempt preference income and deal separately with tax deferral preferences by limiting loss deductions. Under this plan all deferral-created losses would be deductible only from the taxpayer's related business income—as in the example of losses arising from excessive deductions during the early years of a housing investment being deductible only from the profits of other housing projects of the taxpayer—and losses that were not offset in this way would be carried forward for deduction against similar kinds of income in future years. This would stop the sheltering of unrelated income and would encourage the large-scale investor with enough related proj-ects to absorb all current losses; at the same time it would discourage the casual investor who may be presumed to be more interested in tax avoidance than in the management of particular economic ac-tivities. But it would also make it more difficult for new investors to get started.

Table 3-6 shows the estimated revenue effects in 1976 of revising

Table 3-6. Revenue Effects of Revisions in the Minimum Tax for Individuals, by Adjusted Gross Income Class, 1976

Income classes in thousands of dollars

Revenue change and adjusted gross income class	Reduce $30,000 exemption to $5,000	Eliminate deduction for federal taxes	Tax preference income at half the regular rate	
			Present base	Revised base[a]
Revenue change (millions of dollars)	200	200	400	1,600
Percentage distribution of revenue change				
0–3	1.0	*	*	0.2
3–5	0.6	*	0.3	0.2
5–10	4.7	*	0.6	0.8
10–15	4.0	*	0.5	0.7
15–20	8.0	*	0.9	1.6
20–25	5.2	*	0.3	1.2
25–50	20.0	1.0	2.7	6.3
50–100	23.2	9.8	6.8	13.7
100–200	13.8	21.3	10.3	17.3
200–500	6.1	29.2	14.3	19.6
500–1,000	1.5	15.4	11.6	11.1
1,000 and over	0.8	23.3	32.4	20.3
All classes[b]	100.0	100.0	100.0	100.0
Percentage change in tax liabilities				
0–3	4.2[c]	*	0.1	6.1[c]
3–5	0.1	*	0.1	0.2
5–10	0.1	*	*	0.1
10–15	*	*	*	0.1
15–20	0.1	*	*	0.1
20–25	0.1	*	*	0.1
25–50	0.1	*	*	0.3
50–100	0.3	0.2	0.2	1.5
100–200	0.3	0.7	0.6	3.7
200–500	0.3	2.0	1.7	9.2
500–1,000	0.3	3.8	4.9	18.5
1,000 and over	0.1	5.0	11.9	29.7
All classes[b]	0.1	0.2	0.3	1.2

Source: Brookings 1972 tax file, projected to 1976. Figures are rounded.
* Less than 0.05 percent.
a. Exemption is reduced from $30,000 to $5,000 and deduction for taxes is eliminated.
b. Includes negative incomes not shown separately.
c. Percent increase in tax is unusually high because many persons with large incomes have tax shelters that reduce their adjusted gross income to less than $3,000 and pay virtually no individual income tax.

the minimum tax for individuals. Reduction of the $30,000 exemption to $5,000 would increase revenues by $200 million a year; elimination of the deduction for federal taxes would raise another $200 million a year. An increase in the minimum tax to half the ordinary rates would increase revenues $400 million a year. All three changes would raise tax liabilities by $1.6 billion, most of which would come from taxpayers with very high incomes.

Income from Foreign Sources

A notable worldwide economic development in recent years has been the rapid growth of multinational corporations and the proliferation of disputes between them and the different countries in which they operate. Future years, in the view of at least one expert, may witness a series of investment rivalries over the international allocation of productive activity and the division of its economic fruits.[14] Host countries are already active in these struggles, and home countries, among whom the United States is preeminent, can be expected to play an increasingly active role. In such an environment it is not at all surprising that the U.S. tax treatment of business and investment income received by Americans from abroad has become an object of increasingly intense focus.

It is unlikely that many U.S. taxpayers realize the size of their potential stake in the tax treatment of income from foreign sources. In 1972, for example, it is estimated that U.S. corporations had foreign income of $24.4 billion, on which they paid foreign income taxes of $12.0 billion, or 49 percent, but U.S. taxes of only $1.2 billion, or 5 percent. This very low U.S. tax yield results partly from the various tax concessions to be discussed below. But of far greater influence is the standard international practice that countries in which income originates have a prior claim to it and that the taxes they assess should be allowed as credits, fully deductible from any taxes claimed on that income by the corporations' home countries. U.S. direct business investment abroad rose from $49 billion at the end of 1965 to $107 billion at the end of 1973, and the investment expenditures of foreign affiliates of U.S. companies grew at annual rates of 18 percent in

14. C. Fred Bergsten, "Coming Investment Wars?" *Foreign Affairs* (October 1974), pp. 135–52 (Brookings Reprint 299).

1973 and 1974; all this has occasioned increasing doubt about the desirability of the traditional arrangement.

Special Provisions Applicable to Foreign Income

Chief among the special provisions currently applicable to foreign income is the right to defer certain tax liabilities. Whereas domestic corporations and their foreign branches are taxed on all profits currently earned, profits of foreign subsidiaries are taxed by the United States only when remitted as dividends. At that time a credit is allowed for any foreign income taxes paid on the repatriated dividends, up to the amount of the U.S. corporation tax. The deferral privilege has been a substantial advantage to those interested in building up their business operations in low-tax countries. Others have manipulated their corporate structures and accounting reports so as to assign large amounts of reported profits to low-tax subsidiaries. These so-called tax haven operations became blatant enough by 1962 to induce congressional action to restrict them, and this effort was continued in the Tax Reduction Act of 1975.

The result of this legislation is a complex set of rules that constrains U.S. multinationals but leaves many tax deferral privileges intact. Estimates of the revenue cost of these privileges vary widely because of uncertainty about the extent to which their removal would raise the dividend payouts of foreign subsidiaries. These higher dividends would then be subject to foreign withholding taxes, and because of the foreign tax credit U.S. tax collections would be reduced correspondingly. Consider a foreign subsidiary that earns $100 million in a country with a 10 percent corporate tax and a 20 percent dividend withholding tax. If the subsidiary retained all earnings, it would pay a total tax of $10 million, all to the foreign country. If the subsidiary made no change in its retention policy, a shift to full current U.S. taxation would raise its taxes by $38 million (if the U.S. tax rate was 48 percent) and increase Treasury revenues correspondingly. If it retained no earnings, it would remit a net dividend of $72 million to its U.S. parent company, pay a dividend tax of $18 million to the foreign country, and the parent company would owe a net U.S. tax of $20 million. In most cases some intermediate figure would presumably represent the U.S. revenue gain from full current taxation.

U.S. tax deferral on the reinvested profits of foreign subsidiaries both encourages foreign investment at the expense of domestic and reduces U.S. exports by the amount that manufacturing abroad displaces domestic production for export. Treasury and congressional desire to mitigate these effects resulted in the enactment, in the Revenue Act of 1971, of additional deferral privileges for so-called domestic international sales corporations, or DISCs, set up by domestic manufacturers to handle the export of their products. Half of the export income of a DISC is presumed to be distributed to its shareholders, and once in their hands to be subject to current U.S. taxation, but no tax is levied on the other half as long as the DISC continues in existence. This is yet another example of one tax privilege begetting another. DISC operations are growing rapidly, and though the Tax Reduction Act of 1975 repeals DISC privileges for exports of energy products and natural resources subject to depletion, the 1976 revenue cost of DISC privileges is estimated to be $1.5 billion (table 3-7). Whether the 1975 restrictions reflect congressional concern for the conservation of wasting resources more than growing disenchantment with tax deferral privileges in general remains to be seen.

Several other foreign income tax concessions of lesser importance also exist. Since 1942 Western Hemisphere trade corporations, which are domestic companies doing all of their business in the Western Hemisphere and deriving almost all of their income from foreign sources, have enjoyed a 14 percentage point reduction in their U.S. corporate tax rate, and since 1962 U.S. corporations with foreign subsidiaries operating in less developed countries (LDCs) have received preferred treatment over other foreign subsidiaries. One of these advantages is that dividends from LDC corporations are measured for U.S. tax purposes at their net-of-foreign-tax, rather than their gross-of-tax, value. If the corporation in the earlier example that distributed all of its earnings and paid a U.S. tax of $20 million were an LDC corporation, in other words, its U.S. tax base would be $90 million rather than the correct amount of $100 million, and it would owe a U.S. tax of only $15 million (0.48 times $90 million minus $28 million). Still another favored type of U.S. corporation is one operating in U.S. possessions such as Puerto Rico. A further set of concessions allows persons, other than U.S. government employees, who live abroad for at least three years to exclude up to $25,000 of earned income a year from their U.S. tax bases. This is presumably intended to encourage such foreign service, but it may simply relieve employers of salary inducements they would otherwise

**Table 3-7. Revenue Effects of Special Provisions Applying to Foreign
Income of U.S. Citizens and Corporations, Fiscal Year 1976**
Millions of dollars

Provision	Individuals	Corporations	Total
Deferral of tax on domestic inter-			
national sales corporations (DISCs)	...	1,490	1,490
Exclusion of gross-up dividends of less			
developed country corporations	...	55	55
Lower rate for Western Hemisphere			
trade corporations	...	50	50
Exemption for certain income earned			
abroad by U.S. citizens	100	...	100
Deferral of income of controlled			
corporations	...	235	235
Exclusion of income earned in U.S.			
possessions	5	350	355
Total	105	2,180	2,285

Source: U.S. Treasury Department.

have to offer. Even if it raises employee income, it is not clear how
much additional foreign service is thereby induced or how valuable
those increments are to the subsidy-paying U.S. taxpayer. The revenue cost of these special provisions is small but not insignificant (see
table 3-7).

Alternative Revisions

Reform of the U.S. tax treatment of income from foreign sources
involves three major policy options.

1. *Eliminate all foreign tax deferral privileges while retaining the
foreign tax credit in its present form.* This option draws support from
economists who stress worldwide efficiency and equity goals, from
labor groups who argue that tax-subsidized foreign investment reduces U.S. job opportunities, and from advocates of tax simplicity. If
new investment is to flow into the areas of the world where economic
rates of return are highest, it should be neither deterred by extra tax
barriers in those areas nor attracted elsewhere by relatively low tax
burdens. U.S. corporations, therefore, should bear the same tax burdens whether they invest at home or abroad, and elimination of existing tax deferral privileges on foreign income would be an important
step toward that goal. Gains to U.S. labor from the tax reform would
depend on the strength of the shift from foreign to domestic investment by U.S. corporations the reform could be expected to induce,

and they might be longer in coming and more subtle in form than is commonly supposed. Direct investment abroad has been strongly criticized for taking jobs away from U.S. workers by shifting production overseas, but in any well-managed economy the aggregate level of employment would not be affected by such alterations in investment flows. Real wages, on the other hand, tend to rise with the level of the capital stock available, and that should gradually become larger than it would otherwise be in this country if foreign tax deferrals were eliminated.

This first policy option would permit the elimination of the complex rules concerning DISCs, Western Hemisphere trade corporations, LDC corporations, and corporations doing business in U.S. possessions and would remove the profit from artificial tax haven operations. The revenue gain from all of these changes would be $2.3 billion (table 3-7).

In support of retaining foreign-income tax deferrals, on the other hand, it is argued that high foreign investment is essential if this country is to continue developing its world trade comparative advantage in sophisticated technological and management services, that tax subsidies simply offset some of the disadvantages of foreign investment compared to domestic investment, and that higher U.S. tax burdens would impair the ability of foreign subsidiaries to compete in any lower-tax market.

Each side in the debate disputes the importance of the benefits claimed by the other, and few quantitative studies are available to help settle the issue. Much depends on which side should bear the burden of proof. If the case for foreign-income tax deferrals depends on demonstrating that significant economic benefits would be lost under other policy instruments, it has not yet been made. On the other hand, if the case for changing the present tax treatment of income from foreign sources rests on a demonstration that important economic gains and no significant losses would result, it too is far from convincing.

Nor does an appeal for tax equality help much in settling the matter because equal treatment of equals depends on who should be equal to whom. For U.S. taxpayers it is total tax burdens, foreign or domestic, that should be equalized regardless of type or source of income. This would require elimination of all foreign tax deferral privileges, as this first option proposes. For U.S. corporations operating abroad, however, it is likely to be equalization of tax rates on themselves and their foreign competitors that seems most important, and this would require the continuation of current deferral privileges.

It should be stressed that removal of all tax deferral on foreign source income would not truly equalize tax burdens on that income and on domestic income. One source of discrepancy is the constraint that the foreign tax credit be no greater than the U.S. tax rate on equivalent income. This means that investments in high-tax foreign countries may bear greater tax burdens than domestic investments, but to remove the constraint would grant questionable powers to foreign governments to raise their income tax revenues at the expense of the U.S. Treasury. Moreover, most U.S. companies are allowed both an overall and a country-by-country limitation on their foreign tax credit, and any unused credits under either may be carried back for two years and forward for five. These rules give multinational corporations considerable flexibility in the management of their U.S. tax liabilities. The overall limitation, for example, permits them to offset excessive foreign tax burdens against light ones (compared to U.S. tax levels) by pooling their foreign income and taxes before computing their U.S. credit, and the country-by-country calculation may be more favorable to companies with losses in some countries. A stricter set of rules is advocated by some tax reformers, and a step in that direction was taken in the Tax Reduction Act of 1975, which restricted oil companies to use of the overall limitation.

2. *Convert the foreign tax credit into a deduction and eliminate all foreign tax deferral privileges.* This second policy option, which is a radical newcomer in tax reform, rests on the premise that U.S. tax policy should be based not on worldwide economic efficiency goals but on national ones. Although foreign tax credits promote world economic efficiency by tending to equalize net-of-tax rates of return (the ones that motivate private investors) everywhere, part of the gain on foreign investment is captured by the host country in the form of income taxes, and only the remainder flows back to the investing nation. U.S. economic efficiency, in other words, would be maximized by inducing foreign investment only to the point that net-of-foreign-tax rates of return on it were equal to gross-of-tax rates of return at home. This would require conversion of the foreign tax credit into an ordinary tax deduction. It is estimated that the 1976 revenue gain from making this shift would be $7 billion.

Allowing only a deduction for foreign taxes would significantly alter the relative attractiveness of foreign and domestic investment projects. Since it represents a major departure from well-established international traditions and foreign investment will continue to be important for the United States, the change is not one to be undertaken lightly and without due consideration of the likely reaction of other countries. It is not known, however, how great the induced decline in foreign investment might be, nor is it certain that foreign countries would oppose some decline in the growth rate of U.S. investments within their borders. In any case, a deduction would result in the division of the gains from investment tax incentives used by foreign countries between U.S. corporations and the Treasury; a tax credit, in contrast, directs more of those gains to the Treasury.

3. *Maintain the present system with structural improvements.* The most conservative position on the taxation of foreign income favors maintenance of the basic features of the present system but also adoption of certain structural improvements. An important current dispute between the Treasury and some U.S. multinational corporations, for instance, is over the proper allocation of overhead and research and development expenses between their domestic and foreign operations. Frequently these expenses are deducted from domestic gross income since the activities in question are carried out at corporate headquarters and research facilities in this country. A good case can be made, however, for allocating them pro rata to all operations; if this were done, both foreign profits and, more important, the allowable amount of the foreign tax credit would be reduced accordingly. Unless the companies could persuade host governments to recognize the lower foreign profit figure as the proper tax base, and hence to reduce their own tax revenues, the companies would end up with higher net income tax burdens. This is but one of many controversial aspects of the proper division of income and tax claims between countries of origin and countries of destination. The revenue implications of this change are difficult to estimate, but the amount may be substantial.

Another tax concession that should be reconsidered is the present exclusion of incomes earned abroad by U.S. citizens. The conditions under which this provision was adopted have long since been remedied. The result is that some individuals receive handsome tax benefits without contributing anything of value to U.S. objectives at home or abroad. Elimination of the exclusion would increase revenues, at 1976 income levels, by $100 million (table 3-7).

A third source of international tax disputes, particularly in the petroleum industry, is the distinction between foreign taxes, which may be credited in full against U.S. tax liabilities, and royalties and excise taxes, which may only be deducted from the company's tax base and are thus equivalent to a fractional tax credit. The problem is that payments to a foreign government owning natural resources may fall in one category or the other depending on the circumstances. One clear example of a royalty, dealt with in the Tax Reduction Act of 1975, is a payment by a U.S. corporation that has no economic interest in the resource being purchased. A more basic distinction, not now widely applied, would be between a payment specific to the industry in question, which would be a royalty or excise tax entitled only to deductibility status, and a payment based on profits and required of all businesses, which would be a bona fide income tax qualifying for credit status. How much strict adherence to such a rule might raise U.S. tax collections is a question that cannot be answered until experience has tested the effectiveness of the new 1975 rules.

CHAPTER FOUR

Relation between the Corporation and Individual Income Taxes

THE TAXATION of income from corporate sources under the two income taxes, corporation and individual, is a controversial issue among experts that has only recently attracted policy attention in this country. Abroad, the interest has been far greater, and many changes in the relation between the two taxes have been made in recent years.

Basically there are two schools of thought. The integrationists argue that there should be one comprehensive income tax that treats all kinds of income, including that generated by corporations, in exactly the same way. The separatists maintain that a separate corporation income tax is an indispensable part of the fiscal system and that integration of the two income taxes would not necessarily improve the system and might even make it worse. This is not so much an argument between conservatives and liberals—members of both groups can be found on either side—as it is between idealists (integrationists) seeking a perfect tax solution in an imperfect world and pragmatists (separatists) stressing the virtues of second-best solutions. With the corporation tax firmly in place and highly productive of federal revenue, the pragmatists have a strong base from which to operate, but with capital in short supply and with more and more foreign countries attracted to different integration plans, the reformers hope to persuade the United States to follow suit.

Burdens of the Corporation Income Tax

That the present U.S. system of separate corporation and individual income taxes imposes burdens that vary greatly from industry to industry and from shareholder to shareholder is one of the least understood features of federal taxation. For all large corporations the nominal federal tax rate may be taken to be 48 percent (beginning in 1975, the statutory rate is 20 percent on the first $25,000 of taxable profits, 22 percent on the next $25,000, and 48 percent on the rest), but the effective tax rate, measured in relation to true economic income, is little more than 35 percent. This discrepancy is created by the provisions discussed in chapter 3 and is greater for some industries than for others. In 1963, for example, the effective corporate tax rate was only 16 percent for miscellaneous nonmetallic minerals, 18 percent for coal mining, and 20 percent for petroleum refining, but it was 48 percent for tobacco manufacturers, pulp mills, and newspapers. The average for all mining and manufacturing industries was 39 percent, though the nominal rate was 52 percent. Such tax differences are of continuing concern to tax reformers because of their effects on the allocation of resources.

More pertinent to the integrationist-separatist debate are the differences between federal tax rates on income generated by corporations and those on other kinds of income. These differences vary both with the income level of the taxpayer and with the pay-out policies of the corporations in which he owns shares. The simplest case is that of a corporation that distributes all its after-tax profits as dividends. Such profits are taxed twice, once at the corporate level at 48 percent (this ignores for the moment all special provisions) and once at the individual level at the taxpayer's own marginal rate. For a stockholder in the 40 percent tax bracket who owns shares on which $100 of corporate profits have been earned, the total tax burden on those profits would be $68.80, though on any other kind of fully taxable income the tax would be only $40. This is because the corporation pays taxes of $48 and a dividend of $52, on which the shareholder pays an individual income tax of 40 percent, or $20.80.[1] The excess corporate tax burden in this case may then be said to be $28.80 ($68.80 less $40.00). Similarly calculated excess burdens for shareholders in corporations that distribute all their earnings are shown in the first column of table 4-1. It will be noted that the burdens are highest at the bottom of the income scale and lowest at the top.

The calculations are more complicated for retained corporate profits. A shareholder investing in a corporation that retains all its after-tax earnings and reinvests them would expect to see the market value of his shares increase over the long term by at least the amount of the reinvested earnings per share. He would be subject to a capital gains tax if and when he sold his shares, but in this case it is impossible to specify precisely what his total tax would be. The capital gains tax might be paid soon after the profits were earned, it might not be paid for many years, or it might never be paid. It has been estimated that these delays are long enough for the average high-income shareholder to convert a 25 percent capital gains tax rate into a rate equivalent to an immediate levy of only 7 percent. Given these possibilities, table 4-1 shows the range of excess tax burdens that result when corporations retain all their earnings. The excess burdens in the second column apply if no capital gains taxes at all are paid by the shareholders, and those in the third column apply if an immediate long-term capital gains tax is paid. Both sets of excess burdens are heaviest at the bottom of the income scale and become steadily less as the income position of the shareholder increases. Unlike the case for the corporation that distributes all its profits, the burdens become negative—that is, turn from excessive to deficient tax burdens—at high income levels. As the second column shows, this turning point occurs at the 50 percent tax bracket level, when no capital gains tax is ever paid. For shareholders paying an immediate capital gains tax on the earnings reinvested for him by the corporation, however, negative tax burdens occur only at the 70 percent level (see the third column).

The interacting effects of actual corporate pay-out ratios and shareholder marginal tax rates, estimated for the year 1976, are combined in table 4-2. As would be expected from the illustrative calculations

1. This does not take into account the $100 dividend exclusion which, though important to small shareholders, is an insignificant proportion of total dividends paid.

Table 4-1. Additional Burdens of an Unshifted Corporation Income Tax on $100 of Corporation Profit Income[a]

| Marginal individual income tax rates (*percent*) | *Pay-out policy of corporation and capital gains tax paid (dollars)* | | |
	All after-tax corporate profits paid out as dividends (1)	*No profits paid out; no capital gains tax* (2)	*No profits paid out; current long-term capital gains tax* (3)
0	48.00	48.00	48.00
14	41.28	34.00	37.64
20	38.40	28.00	33.20
30	33.60	18.00	25.80
40	28.80	8.00	18.40
50	24.00	−2.00	11.00
60	19.20	−12.00	3.60
70	14.40	−22.00	−3.80

a. The calculations do not take into account the effect of the exclusion of the first $100 of dividends from the individual income tax base.

Column 1 = $48 + 52m - 100m$, column 2 = $48 - 100m$, column 3 = $48 + 26m - 100m$, where m is the marginal tax rate.

Table 4-2. Excess Tax Burdens of the Corporation Income Tax, by Adjusted Gross Income Class, 1976

| Adjusted gross income class (*thousands of dollars*) | *Excess burden as a percent of adjusted AGI*[a] | |
	With no capital gains tax from retained earnings	*With 7 percent capital gains tax from retained earnings*
0–3	2.2	2.4
3–5	2.8	3.1
5–10	1.3	1.5
10–15	0.7	0.8
15–20	0.7	0.8
20–25	0.6	0.7
25–50	0.6	0.8
50–100	−0.6	0.1
100–200	−2.0	−1.1
200–500	−3.5	−2.2
500–1,000	−3.4	−1.7
1,000 and over	−1.2	0.6
Total[b]	0.6	0.9

Source: Brookings 1972 tax file, projected to 1976.

a. Adjusted AGI equals AGI plus retained corporate earnings plus corporate profits tax.

b. Includes negative incomes not shown separately.

in table 4-1, the excess corporate tax burden, expressed as a percentage of total taxpayer income, is greatest in the low income classes and shrinks until it becomes negative at the $50,000 income level. If the potential capital gains taxes on corporate retentions were assumed to be 7 percent, the excess burden would be somewhat greater at all levels but would continue to be negative between $100,000 and $1,000,000. This means that, if the individual and corporation income taxes were integrated, using the same rates as the rates applying to ordinary income under present law (an unlikely assumption since the burden of tax on capital gains from corporate securities would be greatly increased), taxes would be reduced for the lower income classes and increased for the higher income classes. On the other hand, a significant cut in the top-bracket rates could more than offset whatever progressive effect integration might have.

What light do these calculations throw on the integrationist-separatist debate? The first point to note is that the estimates assume that shareholders bear the full burden of the corporation income tax, that no part of its burden is shifted to consumers, workers, or other property owners. While most economists believe that there is some such shifting, there is sufficient support for the argument that shareholders bear a large share of the corporation tax to make the general patterns of the different burdens shown in tables 4-1 and 4-2 significant. They show that a separate corporation profits tax sometimes discriminates against income from corporate sources and sometimes favors it. Such a system fails to meet the standard requirements of horizontal equity. Its rating as part of a progressive, ability-to-pay tax structure is more debatable.

Because corporate share ownership is highly concentrated, a separate proportional corporation tax that is not shifted imposes large burdens on people with high income. This is one of its strong appeals to separatists. On the other hand, as table 4-2 shows, the excess burdens of a separate corporation tax seem to be distributed regressively. Thus full integration would improve the vertical equity of the income tax unless that reform induced reductions in top marginal tax rates that otherwise would not be made.

A tax system employing a separate corporation tax has been strongly criticized for the distortions it produces in the operation of the domestic economic system. It tends to shift resources from high to low rate-of-return uses by placing larger tax burdens on industries in which the corporate form has important economic advantages. It also favors debt financing over equity financing by corporations, discourages capital-intensive methods of production, and makes corporate stock ownership relatively less attractive to those in lower income groups. While the qualitative nature of these effects is clear, their quantitative importance continues to be the subject of much debate.

Still more ambiguous are the burdens that a separate corporation tax imposes on tax-exempt institutions that own corporate shares. Some see these burdens as unwarranted, even capricious, interference with legitimate tax-exemption goals. Others view them as desirable offsets to the general public subsidization of private philanthropy under the individual income tax. The large size of the revenue losses implied by any extension of the benefits of integration to tax-exempt institutions would expose these issues to public controversy. One possible solution would be to extend the present tax on the unrelated business income of tax-exempt institutions to their investment income. It may be argued that public concern for the social benefits of private philanthropic activities requires only that their income from contributions be fully tax-exempt. Investment income in moderate amounts does indeed provide both independence and valuable protection against unforeseen contingencies, but in large amounts it may simply protect the recipient institution from any market test of the value of its activities. A tax on this investment income, then, would not destroy the protected position of heavily endowed philanthropies, but it would reduce their ability to finance activities not directly supported by the public.

Exactly how and to what extent the federal income tax should be applied to the investment income of private philanthropies need not be discussed here.[2] Suffice it to note that, if such a tax should be adopted, there is much to be said for combining its enactment with integration of the corporation and individual income taxes. For private philanthropies the burden of the investment income tax would then be lightened by the benefits conferred on them by integration; for integration proponents and the federal Treasury the large revenue

2. But, in particular, it would be necessary to decide whether the tax would be on gross or net investment income. If the latter, provision would have to be made for the expenses of earning the investment income. This would require the enactment of rules to allocate the outlays of tax-exempt organizations between charitable activities and portfolio management.

losses that might result from extending full integration to all shareholders, including tax-exempt institutions, could be considerably reduced by adoption of the investment income tax.

Viewed in the broader context of the world economy, a separate
corporation tax has more appeal. If the efficient allocation of capital
among countries is an important goal, the two-tax system would provide the simplest basis for the design of national tax systems that
equalize tax burdens on business investment wherever it may be
made. Integrated national tax systems can be designed to achieve the
same goal, but this would involve both additional complexities and
some alterations in well-established conventional rules concerning
nondiscrimination and reciprocity. Corporation tax integration, in
short, promises gains in equity and economic efficiency at some cost
in fiscal efficiency. On the other hand, if national rather than worldwide economic efficiency is given priority, most of the fiscal inefficiencies of integrated tax systems, compared to separate entity ones,
disappear.

Still different considerations arise if the corporation tax has been
shifted forward to consumers in the short run by companies with
sufficient market power to follow what are called administered pricing
policies. In that event some corporate product prices will have risen
substantially, some only slightly, and others not at all. These effects,
which would vary both with the market power of the corporation and
the capital intensity of the industry, bear little or no relation to a
rational plan of consumer taxation. If most of the corporation tax
is indeed borne by consumers, as some believe, a systematically designed federal retail sales or value-added tax would be a much better
way of achieving the same policy goals.

Finally, whether an integrated tax would provide greater equity
than the present system depends on the level and configuration of the
tax rates adopted. Separatists are deeply concerned that the top
bracket rates might be adjusted downward and this could make the
move to an integrated tax regressive. Congressional reluctance to
raise the capital gains rates to equal the regular rates suggests that
this concern is not without foundation. Integrationists, however,
doubt that integration would create any additional pressure for top-
bracket rate reductions. In their view, it is the existence of a separate
corporation tax that helps keep down capital gains tax rates.

The case against a separate corporation profits tax is thus a mixed one. To change the present U.S. system, reformers will have to convince the public of two things—first, that the economic gains from shifting to a more integrated income tax system are significant and, second, that the revenues lost by eliminating the separate corporation tax can and will be replaced by equitable sources of federal funds. Three policy options deserve consideration.

Alternative Policy Options

The first two options represent a partial integration of the corporation and individual income taxes, based on the proposition that only distributed corporate earnings deserve tax relief.[3] The third option extends this proposition to cover retained earnings as well, and in the process achieves full integration of the two income taxes.

Exempt Dividends from the Corporation Income Tax

Exempting from the corporation income tax dividends paid out would convert that tax into one on retained earnings only and would achieve horizontal equity as far as distributed corporate income is concerned. It is a logical extension of the split-rate corporation tax systems that exist in a number of countries. For instance, Germany, which abandoned the separate entity system in 1953, taxes retained profits at 51 percent and distributed profits at 15 percent.

Adopting this option would eliminate all of the excess tax burdens for corporations that fully distribute (shown in the first column of table 4-1), reduce those for other distributing companies, but leave unchanged those for the nondistributing companies (shown in the second and third columns of the table). The 1976 revenue cost of the reform would range from $18 billion if there were no changes in corporate dividend policies to $27 billion if dividends were doubled, with most of the tax reduction going to the higher income classes.[4] It would lessen the present tax discrimination against equity (as opposed to debt) financing, and it would presumably make investment in corporate shares more attractive to individuals. This would happen

3. All the options assume that the dividend exclusion would be eliminated. The revenue gain would be $340 million at 1976 income levels.

4. The distribution by income class would be similar to the distribution of all the special corporation tax provisions discussed in chapter 3. See, for example, table 3-4, columns 2 and 5.

directly if corporations used part of their tax savings to pay higher dividends and indirectly if their additional retained profits generated increases in the market value of their shares. The policy would encourage dividend distribution and might therefore reduce corporate savings, but it would generate corporate tax reductions that could be retained as well as distributed. It would of course be necessary to increase the rates of other taxes or to enact a new tax source to raise the lost revenues.

All integration plans encounter difficulties in their treatment of international income flows. Basically this is because integration aims at a residence-oriented system of taxing business income in a world that is strongly origin-oriented. If dividends were excluded from the corporation tax base, the problem would be the treatment of dividends paid by U.S. corporations to foreign shareholders. Unless there was countervailing action, these would bear lower U.S. tax burdens than they do now, and under existing foreign tax credit laws most of the benefit would accrue to foreign governments rather than to the shareholders. The United States could seek to raise its withholding tax rates on dividends flowing abroad, but these rates are set by tax treaties and changes in them would require agreement by all parties. After adopting its split-rate system, Germany, for instance, was able to negotiate compensating withholding tax rate increases with several countries, though not with the United States, which held firmly to the standard reciprocity rule that withholding rates for developed countries should be the same in the two contracting countries.

In response to such difficulties it has been suggested that a better criterion of intercountry equity would be one that sought equality not in nominal tax rates but rather in the effective level of taxes on foreign investment in the two countries. Under such a rule the country with a relatively low corporation tax would employ a relatively high withholding tax on dividends and vice versa.

Finally, this partial approach to integration automatically extends its benefits to all low income persons, whether taxable or not, and to tax-exempt institutions. The granting of additional tax benefits to the latter is both controversial and costly in federal revenue and might, as suggested above, provide an occasion for some broadening of the existing tax on the unrelated business income of private philanthropies.

Grossed-up Dividend Tax Credit

Like the first option, adopting this proposal could achieve integration for distributed corporate profits, but the necessary adjustments would be made at the individual rather than the corporation level. Each shareholder would gross up his dividend receipt to include the corporation tax already paid on it, add the grossed-up amount to his other taxable income, compute the tax thereon, and then deduct the corporation tax as a credit. A $52 dividend, for example, would be grossed up to $100 to include the $48 corporate tax, and if the shareholder's marginal tax rate were, say, 35 percent, he would have $13 ($48 minus $35) to deduct from the taxes due on his other income. A shareholder with a 48 percent bracket would come out even, and an investor in the 70 percent bracket would owe another $22 on the dividend payment. Integration for distributed income from corporate sources would require use of a refundable credit, payable in cash to shareholders with insufficient tax liabilities to absorb the credit. If the credit were refundable to individuals, tax-exempt institutions owning corporate stock (which are in the same position) would expect to be treated the same way, thus raising the revenue loss significantly unless some compensating tax on those institutions' investment income were enacted at the same time.

Use of a dividend credit would also raise the difficult question of the extent to which it should be given on dividends paid out of profits not fully taxed at the corporate level. If the credit is viewed solely as a means of alleviating the double taxation of dividends, only partial credits should be given on partially taxed corporate income that is distributed. This is extremely complicated to accomplish in practice, although both France and Great Britain, which adopted dividend tax credits in 1965 and 1973 respectively, make some adjustments by levying an additional "advance corporation tax" on dividends paid out of partially taxed profits. Alternatively, if the undertaxation of certain corporate profits is viewed as an incentive measure whose effects should be passed through to the stockholders, a full tax credit at the nominal corporation tax rate is the appropriate solution.

Two kinds of international tax problems would be created by the adoption of a grossed-up dividend credit. The first is whether the credit should be extended to individual U.S. investors who own shares

in foreign corporations. The Treasury would not be enthusiastic about giving U.S. shareholders credit for taxes paid to other countries, and the revenue cost could be high if those shareholders chose to invest mainly in high-tax foreign countries. However, if the credit was not extended to shares in foreign corporations, U.S. investors would find domestic corporate shares more attractive than foreign and some loss in worldwide economic efficiency would presumably result. Most countries adopting the crediting device do not extend it to shares in foreign countries, so this loss in efficiency is already being realized. The second problem is whether to extend the credit to individual foreign investors owning shares in U.S. corporations. Failure to do so might be regarded as a violation of the international equity rule of equal treatment of equals, but doing so would raise the revenue cost of the proposal, a cost that would have to be weighed against the potential investment gains. France began extending its credit to foreign portfolio investors in 1967 through bilateral treaty agreements and by 1973 had completed arrangements with nine countries, including the United States. On the other hand, the United Kingdom does not provide a dividend credit to foreign shareholders in U.K. corporations.

Dividend tax credit and gross-up plans, then, come in many varieties, each with its own revenue cost. At 1976 dividend levels, the full gross-up procedure with the credit to individuals—but not to tax-exempt organizations—for the imputed corporation tax paid would cost $15 billion a year. The largest percentage reductions in tax would go to the lowest and highest income classes; because stockholdings are highly concentrated in the highest classes, nearly 50 percent of the reductions would go to those with incomes above $25,000 (see table 4-3).

Eliminate the Corporation Profits Tax and Tax Corporation Profits under the Individual Income Tax

Full integration of the corporation and individual income taxes may be achieved in one of two ways. First, the corporation income tax could be eliminated and shareholders would be taxed at regular rates on their accrued capital gains. Since the retained earnings of corporations would be reflected (to some degree, at least) in the value of the corporate shares, in effect they would be subject to personal income tax in this way. This solution is probably not practical for two

Table 4-3. Revenue Effects of Plan to Provide Full Credit for the Corporation Tax Paid on Dividends, by Adjusted Gross Income Class, 1976
Income classes in thousands of dollars; tax amounts in billions of dollars

Adjusted gross income class	Present tax	Tax under dividend gross-up plan		Tax reduction		
		Tax before credit[a]	Tax after credit[b]	Amount	As a per- cent of present tax	Percentage distribu- tion
0–3	*	0.1	−0.3	0.4	890.5[c]	2.5
3–5	1.1	1.3	−0.1	1.0	86.7[c]	6.3
5–10	10.8	11.2	8.9	1.9	17.4	12.3
10–15	20.0	20.6	18.4	1.6	8.1	10.7
15–20	23.6	24.3	21.9	1.7	7.2	11.2
20–25	18.5	18.9	17.5	1.0	5.5	6.6
25–50	30.3	32.6	27.3	3.0	10.0	19.8
50–100	15.3	18.0	13.0	2.3	14.9	14.8
100–200	7.6	9.4	6.5	1.1	14.0	7.0
200–500	3.5	4.8	2.9	0.6	17.3	4.0
500–1,000	1.0	1.5	0.8	0.2	23.2	1.5
1,000 and over	1.1	1.7	0.8	0.3	25.4	1.9
All classes[d]	132.9	144.3	117.7	15.3	11.5	100.0

Source: Brookings 1972 tax file, projected to 1976. Figures are rounded.
* Less than $50 million.
a. Tax at 1975 tax rates and exemptions on adjusted gross income plus corporate tax assumed to have been paid on dividends.
b. Tax after allowing for a refundable credit for corporate taxes assumed to have been paid on dividends.
c. Percent reduction in tax is unusually large because persons with incomes of less than $3,000 pay virtually no individual income tax.
d. Includes negative incomes not shown separately.

reasons: one is that the capital gains rates would have to be raised substantially to avoid a large revenue loss; the other is that the taxation of accrued capital gains on nontraded equities would be fraught with difficulties.

A second alternative would be to allocate retained corporate earnings to shareholders and tax them at the regular individual income tax rates. The mechanics might be handled in the way recommended by the Royal Commission on Taxation (the Carter Commission) of Canada in 1966. Their plan was to set a withholding rate on corporate earnings at the top individual marginal tax rate, recommended to be 50 percent, and allow corporations to allocate retained profits to shareholders for tax purposes. This would be done by sending each shareholder a statement showing his pro rata share of retained profits and the tax withheld on that share. The total would be included in the shareholder's taxable income for the year in question, the withheld tax would be deducted from the total tax due on that income, and the cost basis of his shares would be written up by the amount of the profit allocation. Since all but top-bracket shareholders would enjoy tax reductions (or cash rebates if their tax liabilities were less than the corporate withholding tax) under this procedure, allocations could be expected to be virtually universal and each year's retained profits would be taxed at the correct marginal tax rate for each shareholder. Moreover, the write-up in the cost basis of his shares, required to avoid double taxation of retained profits and any future capital gains generated by them, would significantly reduce the lock-in effects to which the shareholder might otherwise be subject.

If the allocation plan were adopted in the United States without any other change in the tax law, it would be necessary to keep the top bracket rates at or close to present levels to avoid reducing the progressivity of the income taxes. This means that the corporate withholding rate would have to be set at or close to the present 70 percent rate. The effect would be to reduce the earnings available either for retention or for dividend distribution to no more than about 30 percent of the corporation's before-tax profits. For the average corporation, this small margin left after the withholding tax had been paid would require substantial reductions in corporate saving or dividend payments, or both. Stockholders would ultimately receive more, because most of them would be eligible for refunds from the government for the difference between their marginal tax rates and the corporate withholding rate. However, there would be no way for corporations to avoid reductions in their retained earnings, and in some cases the reductions would be substantial. Integrationists who believe that the tax system should not encourage corporate saving would approve this result; others might have strong reservations.

The allocation plan would encounter all the international tax problems mentioned above, but in a more intense form because it would represent full rather than partial integration of the corporation and individual income taxes. Even if all major countries adopted full integration at the same time, there would be controversy, familiar to all students of state and local taxation, over the relative rights of capital-exporting and capital-importing countries to tax international business income flows. If the United States were to adopt full integration on its own, debate would center on how much tax relief this country should extend either to the shareholders of other countries

**Table 4-4. Estimate of the Revenue Loss from Full Integration
of the Corporation and Individual Income Taxes, 1976**
Billions of dollars

Item	Revenue loss
Present tax	
1. Economic income of regular stock companies[a]	137.7
2. Federal corporation income taxes paid	52.0
3. Dividends of regular stock companies	38.0
4. Dividends received by shareholders filing income tax returns (76 percent of line 3)[b]	28.9
5. Tax on dividends	9.0
6. Total tax on corporate-source income (line 2 plus line 5)	61.0
Tax under full integration	
7. Corporate profits imputed to individual shareholders (76 percent of line 1)	104.7
8. Tax on corporate source income[c]	41.6
9. Revenue loss from full integration (line 6 minus line 8)	19.4
10. Tax on corporate-source income of tax-exempt organizations[d]	12.5
11. Revenue loss from full integration for shareholders only (line 9 minus line 10)[e]	6.9

Sources: Authors' estimates; lines 5, 8, and 11 computed from the Brookings tax file for 1972, projected to 1976.

a. Excludes state-local corporation profits taxes and profits of tax-exempt organizations.

b. The other 24 percent of dividends flows to tax-exempt organizations.

c. Tax at present individual income tax rates, net after subtraction of estimated tax now paid by individuals on capital gains that reflect corporate retentions.

d. Assuming 24 percent of corporate tax is paid by tax-exempt organizations.

or to its own shareholders who invest in foreign companies. Both procedures would be costly in terms of Treasury revenue, but failure to adopt one or the other would inject potentially distorting tax considerations into international investment markets.

Even if the international aspects of full integration were settled with little or no loss of revenue, the change would be costly. As table 4-4 indicates, total federal taxes on corporate source income are estimated at $61 billion in 1976, but full integration for all shareholders would yield only $42 billion at present individual income tax rates. But if the tax reductions extended to tax-exempt organizations by integration were eliminated by taxing their corporate income at the 1976 effective corporation tax rate, an additional $12 billion would be collected and the revenue loss would be reduced to $7 billion. An alternative option, already noted, would be to levy a tax on the entire investment income—interest as well as dividends—of tax-exempt institutions. On the other hand, those who believe that full integration would be politically feasible only if marginal tax rates at the individual level were reduced at the same time should expect even larger revenue losses. Some would regard such losses as proving the futility of any attempt at full integration; others would use them to argue the folly of *not* moving at once to full integration since they indicate that corporate income is overtaxed at present. The potential revenue loss from integration could, of course, be made up in any number of different ways.

This, in any case, is not the crux of the matter. At the cost of considerable short-run dislocation and readjustment, individual and corporation income tax integration promises equity and efficiency gains of potentially large but uncertain dimensions. Only if these long-run gains outweigh the short-run costs is the game worth the candle, and on this question there is still much difference of opinion.

CHAPTER FIVE

The Payroll Tax, Estate and Gift Taxes, and Consumption Taxes

THE TYPES of questions that concern the other taxes in the tax system—payroll taxes, estate and gift taxes, and consumption taxes—are very different from those raised in connection with the income taxes. Nevertheless, the problems are no less difficult and also involve tax equity and economic efficiency.

The Payroll Tax for Social Security

Since its inception in 1935 the social security system has been financed by a payroll tax. This method of financing was selected on the principle that the workers were buying insurance and that a tax on their earnings would be an appropriate premium. At present, the payroll tax for social security programs amounts to 11.7 percent of earnings up to a maximum of $14,100 in 1975 and $15,300 in 1976, half of which is paid by the employer and half by the employee. Most economists believe that not only the portion paid by the employee but all or a major share of the payroll tax paid by the employer as well falls eventually on the worker (either by substituting for larger wage increases or inflating prices).[1]

The insurance idea is credited with the widespread acceptance of social security as a permanent government program and continues to have a strong hold on the thinking of the Social Security Administration and the congressional tax committees, as well as the public. But the analogy to insurance has been greatly weakened by the way the system has developed. Present beneficiaries receive far larger payments than the taxes they paid would entitle them to under a regular insurance plan—a situation that will continue indefinitely as long as Congress raises benefits as prices and wages continue to rise. The social security trust funds do not have balances sufficient to pay much more than about one year's benefits, and in recent years the policy has been to conduct the system roughly on a pay-as-you-go basis. Thus the payroll taxes paid by workers are not being stored up or invested but are being paid out currently as benefits. When benefits promised to people now working become due, the funds for their payments will come from tax revenues at that future date.[2]

Since the payroll tax is levied beginning with the first dollar of earnings, it places a very heavy burden on low-income workers, and becomes regressive when earnings exceed the maximum taxable level. Moreover, the payroll tax does not apply to income from property, which is concentrated in the higher income classes. By contrast, the individual income tax largely exempts the poor from taxation, applies to property income as well as earnings, and is progressive above the minimum taxable levels. The regressive effect of the payroll tax is illustrated in figure 5-1, which shows the burden of the payroll and individual income taxes at various income levels for a family of four with one earner whose income is all earned. For such families, the payroll tax is a larger burden than the income tax for earnings up to

1. See Joseph A. Pechman, Henry J. Aaron, and Michael K. Taussig, *Social Security: Perspectives for Reform* (Brookings Institution, 1968), pp. 175–78; and John A. Brittain, *The Payroll Tax for Social Security* (Brookings Institution, 1972), pp. 21–81.

2. This does not mean that payroll tax rates must increase as the ratio of retired persons to population increases. It can be shown that a system with benefits increasing in proportion to wages can be financed without increasing tax rates, so long as the sum of the rates of growth in productivity and in the labor force is at least equal to the rate of growth in the number of retired persons.

Figure 5-1. Effective Rates of Individual Income and Payroll Taxes for a Married Couple with Two Children, by Income Level, 1975[a]

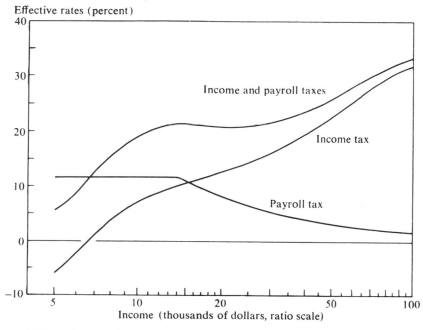

Effective rates (percent)

Income and payroll taxes

Income tax

Payroll tax

Income (thousands of dollars, ratio scale)

a. All income is assumed earned. Income tax is net after credit of 10 percent of earned income up to $4,000, phasing out to zero between $4,000 and $8,000.

$15,000.[3] In fact, the payroll tax is the larger tax for more than half of all wage earners. In combination, the two taxes—which account for about three-quarters of total federal receipts—rise as a percentage of income up to $12,000, stay at about the same percentage between $12,000 and $30,000, and rise again above $30,000. The range within which the effective rates are roughly proportional includes about 50 percent of all family units.

If, as many argue, the payroll tax of any particular person cannot be regarded as a contribution to the benefit he will ultimately receive, there is no reason for imposing such a large share of the burden of financing the nation's social security system on the poor and near poor; like any other government program, the system should be financed by a progressive rather than a regressive tax source. The opposing view holds that the connection between payroll taxes paid and

3. This assumes that the payroll tax paid by the employer is borne by workers.

later benefits received, however tenuous, is still an important feature of the system which protects it against benefit cuts for budgetary reasons. The equity gains to taxpayers from more progressive payroll taxation must therefore be balanced against the potential equity losses to beneficiaries from lowered support levels.

Several different approaches might be taken to achieve progressivity. One would be to abolish the payroll tax and substitute receipts from other federal tax sources. This would require substantial increases in tax rates; for example, both the individual and the corporation income tax rates would have to be raised by an average of over 40 percent to recover the revenue lost from eliminating the payroll tax. Another method would be to make the payroll tax itself progressive by lifting the maximum taxable earnings level and introducing the type of exemption and low-income allowance now used in the individual income tax.[4] Still a third method, which would not fully meet the criterion of progressivity but would alleviate the burden on the poor, was adopted in 1975. Under it, a refundable tax credit of 10 percent of earned income up to a maximum of $400 is provided for people with children. The credit is phased down from $400 to zero as earned income (or adjusted gross income, if greater) increases from $4,000 to $8,000. Extension of this credit to people without children would offset almost entirely both the employer and employee taxes on earnings of $4,000 or less.[5]

The estimated revenue effects in 1976 of various combinations of such reforms are given in table 5-1.[6] Introduction of a per capita exemption of $900 plus an allowance of $2,000 would cost a large

4. The taxable earnings ceiling now determines the maximum amount of wages that is credited to the individual for the purpose of computing his retirement benefit. If the ceiling were lifted, it would be necessary to make this decision without reference to the tax. For example, either the maximum wages to be credited could be set at two or three times the median wage level or benefits could be computed on the basis of total wages and salaries. At present, the maximum benefit rate for wages of more than $1,000 a month is 20 percent. To avoid inordinately high benefits for high-salaried people, the benefit rate for wages more than two or three times the median wage would have to be much smaller.

5. With a combined rate of 11.7 percent on earnings up to the maximum taxable limit, the 10 percent refundable credit offsets about 85 percent (10 divided by 11.7 times 100) of the combined tax up to $4,000 of earnings.

6. The estimates are based on the assumption that the 10 percent refundable credit on earnings up to $4,000 would be repealed, since any one of the revisions in table 5-1 would be more generous than the credit.

Table 5-1. Revenue Effects of Various Revisions in the Social Security Payroll Tax, 1976
Billions of dollars

Reform provision	Change in revenue
Portion paid by employee[a]	
1. Retain taxable earnings ceiling and	
a. Introduce a $2,000 allowance plus a $900 per capita exemption	−17.2
b. Same as 1a, but phase out allowance and exemption by $1 for every $2 of earnings[b]	−7.7
2. Remove taxable ceiling and	
a. Introduce allowance and exemption as in 1a	−8.2
b. Introduce phase-out allowance and exemption as in 1b	2.3
Portion paid by employer	
3. Retain taxable earnings ceiling and	
a. Introduce allowance and exemption as in 1a	−17.0
b. Introduce phased-out allowance and exemption as in 1b	−6.7
4. Remove taxable earnings ceiling and	
a. Introduce allowance and exemption as in 1a	−10.9
b. Introduce phased-out deduction and exemption as in 1b[b]	−0.3
Full reform[a]	
5. Remove taxable earnings ceiling and introduce allowance and exemption as in 1a for both employer and employee contribution	−19.1
6. Same as 5 plus an increase in payroll tax rate of 1.7 percentage points	1.5

Source: Brookings 1972 tax file, projected to 1976.
a. Includes taxes paid by the self-employed; assumes individual income tax earned-income credit enacted in 1975 is eliminated.
b. Phase-out begins at the level of income equal to the $900 per capita exemption plus the $2,000 low-income allowance.

amount of revenue[7]—$17.2 billion if applied only to the part of the tax paid by the employee and almost double that amount if applied also to the employer tax.[8] However, this revenue loss could be reduced substantially if the allowance and exemption were phased out. With a phase-out of $1 for every $2 of earnings, the loss would be cut to $7.7 billion. On the other hand, removal of the taxable earnings ceiling would raise $9 billion, making the net cost with a full allowance and exemption only about $8.2 billion. The same changes for the employer tax would have roughly similar effects. The combined effect of introducing a full allowance and exemption and removing

7. These are the amounts required to bring the minimum taxable level approximately to the estimated poverty lines for 1975.
8. The difference between the two sets of estimates is due primarily to the inclusion as an employee tax of the taxes paid by the self-employed.

Table 5-2. Effective Payroll Tax Rates under Present Law and Rates under a Reformed Payroll Tax System, by Adjusted Gross Income Class, 1976

Adjusted gross income class (thousands of dollars)	Effective rates[a] (percent of income)		Change in effective rates
	Present law	Full reform[b]	
0–3	9.6	0.3	−9.3
3–5	7.8	2.3	−5.5
5–10	9.9	6.1	−3.8
10–15	10.9	8.6	−2.3
15–20	10.3	9.9	−0.4
20–25	9.2	10.7	1.5
25–50	6.6	10.8	4.2
50–100	2.8	9.5	6.7
100–200	1.4	8.7	7.3
200–500	0.6	6.6	6.0
500–1,000	0.2	4.2	4.0
1,000 and over	0.1	2.6	2.5
All classes[c]	8.8	8.8	0.0

Source: Brookings 1972 tax file, projected to 1976.

a. Effective rates are the total of taxes paid by employees, employers, and the self-employed as a percent of adjusted gross income.

b. Full reform includes a low-income allowance of $2,000 and per capita exemption of $900, removal of the taxable earnings ceiling, an increase in the payroll tax rate of 1.7 percentage points, and elimination of the individual income tax earned-income credit enacted in 1975.

c. Includes negative incomes not shown separately.

the taxable earnings ceiling for both taxes is a revenue loss of $19.1 billion. This amount of revenue could be raised by an increase in the payroll tax rate of somewhat less than 1.7 percentage points.

The effect of full reform of the payroll tax on the progressivity of the tax system would be substantial (see table 5-2). Effective tax rates would be reduced for families with incomes below $20,000 and increased for families above that level. Under present law, the payroll tax is slightly progressive for income up to $15,000, and then becomes regressive. Under the reformed system, it would be progressive up to the $50,000 level. Regressivity sets in beyond that point because earnings decline sharply as a percentage of income for families at the top of the income scale.

Estate and Gift Taxes

The estate tax is levied on the amount of property transferred from one person to another by bequest. The gift tax is levied on the total amount of gifts made by any individual since 1932.

The major purpose of taxing gifts and bequests is to reduce the inequality of the distribution of wealth. They are also regarded as a better method of taxing the wealthy than the income taxes because they may have less adverse effects on economic incentives. Despite their advantages on social and economic grounds, estate and gift taxes amount to a small proportion of federal revenues. In fiscal year 1976 they are expected to generate only about 1.5 percent of the tax receipts of the federal government.

The low yield is attributable to the structural features of these taxes. The exemptions are $60,000 for the estate tax and $3,000 a year for each donee plus a lifetime exclusion of $30,000 under the gift tax, and rates reach a maximum of 77 percent under the estate tax and 57.75 percent under the gift tax. But these rates apply to only a small fraction of the total property transfers between generations. It is estimated that less than a quarter of the total wealth owned by those who die in any one year is subject to the estate and gift taxes.

The structural defects of the two taxes have an unequal effect on different people. Proper planning can greatly reduce or even eliminate the liability of a person under the estate and gift taxes; another equally rich person, who for business or other reasons may not have been able to arrange the disposition of his estate so as to avoid taxes, might be subject to the full impact of the high rates. Unless the structure of the two taxes were revised, rate increases would aggravate these inequalities. The major problems are (1) the treatment of transfers of husbands and wives, (2) separate taxation of gifts and estates, and (3) the use of trusts to escape taxation of gifts and estates.

Transfers by Husbands and Wives

At the present time a deduction is allowed under the estate tax for the amount of property transferred to a surviving spouse, up to half the estate. In the case of gifts by one spouse to another, only half the gift is taxable, and gifts to third persons are treated as though half were made by each spouse.[9] In effect, the estate tax exemption for married couples is doubled from $60,000 to $120,000, the annual

---

9. These rules apply to non-community property states. In community property states, property acquired during marriage by husband and wife (except property from gifts or inheritance) belongs equally to each spouse, so there is no need for special arrangements for gifts between spouses or to third parties from community property.

exclusion under the gift tax is doubled from $3,000 to $6,000 for each donee, and the lifetime gift tax exemption is doubled from $30,000 to $60,000. Despite this generous treatment, there are substantial differences in the taxes imposed in community property and non-community property states because the total amount of tax depends not only on the amount of property owned by each spouse but also on when and where they die or make gifts.[10]

There are a number of ways to resolve these problems, but each presents problems of its own. One possibility is to consider husbands and wives as a single taxable unit for purposes of the estate and gift taxes. Transfers between spouses would not be taxed, but transfers to others would be taxed on a cumulative basis for estate and gift tax purposes, with the final installment to be collected on the death of the second spouse. While this proposal would equalize the taxes of married couples regardless of how they disposed of their wealth, it might not be considered equitable to combine the wealth of both spouses for tax purposes if it is separately inherited or accumulated.

A second proposal would eliminate the tax on all transfers between spouses without accumulating the estates of husbands and wives. The advantage of this approach is that married couples could arrange their affairs in any way they wished, but it would substantially reduce the yield of the estate tax, at least in the short run.

A third proposal would provide an exemption of a fixed amount, say, $250,000, on transfers between spouses in addition to the usual exemption of $60,000. However, to be fair to couples in community property and non-community property states, this proposal would require overturning the community property laws and taxing the estate in such states to the spouse who earned the wealth. Such a proposal might raise a considerable amount of revenue, but it would be strongly resisted by congressional representatives of the community property states.

10. Unlike the income splitting provision under the income tax, the estate splitting provision did not achieve equality in the estate taxes of married couples living in community and non-community property states. For example, if the wife dies first and leaves her property to the children, her estate is taxable on half of the property accumulated by the husband in a community property state, and his estate is taxable on the second half when he dies. In the non-community property state, assuming the husband accumulated the estate, his entire estate is taxable when he dies; because the rates are graduated, his estate pays more than the two estates in the community property state.

Separate Taxation of Estates and Gifts

A taxpayer pays a lower amount of tax on gifts than on estates for four reasons. First, the gift tax rates are 25 percent lower than the estate tax rates. Second, the estate is split between the estate and gift tax brackets, thus avoiding the full impact of graduation in each rate schedule. Third, using gifts permits the individual to take advantage of the annual $3,000 per donee exclusion and the lifetime exemption of $30,000 in addition to the $60,000 estate tax exemption. Fourth, the amount of gift tax paid is not included in the base of the gift tax, whereas the estate tax is computed on the basis of the total amount transferred, including that part used to pay the tax. Thus a carefully drawn plan of wealth distribution can greatly reduce the taxes that a person must pay on the property he transfers to his heirs.

The remedy for this problem is to unify the estate and gift taxes into one tax, a variant of which has recently been adopted in the United Kingdom. Under this system gifts would continue to be taxed on a cumulated basis, and bequests would in effect be regarded as the last gift during the life of the decedent. Tax would also be paid on a cumulated basis, with the estate tax being regarded as the final installment. Under this type of unified tax, there would be one set of exemptions. Since the separate exemptions are now $60,000 for the estate tax and $30,000 for the gift tax, the combined exemption would presumably be between $60,000 and $90,000. The exclusion for lifetime gifts could be retained at the present $3,000 per donee per year, or perhaps even increased somewhat.

Generation Skipping through Trusts

The most difficult problem of estate and gift taxation results from the use of trusts to transfer property from one generation to later generations. For example, a man might set up a trust to pay out the income from his property to his wife for her life and then to the children for their lives; at the death of the children the trust would be dissolved and the property distributed to the grandchildren. The property would be subject to estate tax when it was set up, but there would be no tax when one of the income beneficiaries succeeded another or when it was terminated. This device is used by wealthy people to avoid estate taxes for one or more generations.

Since trust property tends to go to the same heirs as property transferred outright, there seems to be no good reason for permitting transfers through trusts to escape death taxation. But it is not easy to equalize the estate taxes on the two types of transfers because of the difficulty of measuring the value of the trust to an income beneficiary.

The most direct method of taxing trusts would be to treat the income beneficiaries of a trust as if they were the owners. Then the trust would be taxable as part of the estate of the income beneficiary when he died. Another approach would be to impose a separate tax on the value of the property in which the decedent had a life interest. This method would have greater simplicity, but it would not fully remove the tax advantage of using the trust device. A third method would be to impose a separate tax either on the property when it was placed in trust or when the trust dissolved. The additional tax would be a substitute for the taxes that should be imposed whenever one income beneficiary succeeds another and when the trust terminates. However, the separate tax would probably be arbitrary and would bear little relation to the tax that would be paid on similar property transferred from generation to generation without the use of the trust device.

An Accessions Tax

Still another possibility for reforming the death tax would be to switch to the accessions tax principle. In this form of taxation, the tax is levied on the heirs rather than on the one making the bequest. The tax would be cumulative for each individual on his total lifetime acquisitions, regardless of whether they were received as gifts or bequests.[11] In principle, gifts and bequests are income to the recipient and therefore should be taxed along with his other income under the individual income tax (with averaging to moderate the effect of bunching income in a single year). However, if present practice under the estate and gift taxes is followed, accessions would be subject to a separate tax rate schedule.

The accessions tax is appealing on a number of grounds. First, it seems more reasonable to tax the person who receives gifts and bequests than to tax the donor, since the recipient ultimately enjoys the property from which the tax is paid. Second, the accessions tax would

---

11. The inheritance tax is similar to the accessions tax, except that it applies only to receipts from bequests and is not cumulative. This type of tax is regarded as less equitable than the accessions tax, because it would permit wholesale tax avoidance through gifts.

Table 5-3. Revenue Effects of Reforms of the Estate and Gift Taxes, 1975[a]
Billions of dollars

Reform provision	Amount of revenue
1. Transfers between husbands and wives[b]	
a. Complete exemption of transfers between spouses	−0.5
b. Complete exemption of transfers between spouses, but cumulative taxation of transfers by husbands and wives to others	1.6
c. Provide exemption of $250,000 for transfers between spouses[c]	1.0
2. Integrate the estate and gift taxes[b]	0.3
3. Transfers in generation-skipping trusts	
a. Tax the trust under the estate tax as if it were the property of the income beneficiaries	0.7
b. Impose a separate tax of 25 percent on the value of the property of which the decedent was an income beneficiary	0.6
c. Place a separate tax of 25 percent on trusts either when they are created or when they are dissolved	0.5
4. Changes in rates and exemptions	
a. Increase exemption under the estate tax to $100,000 and lifetime exemption under the gift tax to $50,000	−0.8
b. Reduce exemption under the estate tax to $40,000 and lifetime exemption under the gift tax to $20,000	0.6
c. Reduce estate and gift tax rates across the board by 10 percent	−0.6
5. Combinations of reforms	
a. 1b, 2, 3a, 4a, and 4c	1.2
b. 1a, 2, 3c, 4a, and 4c	−1.1
6. Substitute an accessions tax for the estate and gift taxes[b]	
a. With exemption of $90,000 for all lifetime acquisitions	−2.2
b. With exemption of $50,000 for all lifetime acquisitions	−1.4

Source: Estimates by Gerald R. Jantscher.
a. Most of these reforms would have their full effect on revenues only after many years. The figures here are the increases or decreases in 1975 tax collections that would have been experienced if the reforms had been enacted some time ago.
b. Assumes the present estate and gift tax rates would apply.
c. Assumes community property is taxed to the spouse who earned or inherited the wealth.

encourage a wider distribution of wealth. Third, it would automatically equalize the taxes on transfers during life and at death.

Although appealing in principle, the accessions tax has never been seriously considered by the Congress. Unless exemptions were reduced drastically, the accessions tax would raise less revenue than the estate and gift taxes. And the accessions tax would not provide any better solution than the estate and gift taxes to the problems of taxing property transferred through trusts.

Table 5-3 summarizes the revenue effects of these revisions in the estate and gift taxes. The total revenue gain from all the revisions could amount to as much as $2.5 billion a year. As indicated in the table, an increase in the estate tax exemption from $60,000 to $100,000 and in the gift tax exemption from $30,000 to $50,000 would reduce revenues by $800 million, and a 10 percent reduction in tax rates would cost $600 million. Although the gain in equity could be substantial, the revenue potential of structural reform in the estate and gift taxes is not large, particularly if accompanied by exemption increases and rate reductions.[12]

Federal Consumption Taxes

Consumption taxes in the United States account for a small proportion of total revenue. The federal, state, and local governments all use selective excises, which are taxes imposed on the sales of a particular commodity or group of commodities; only the states and some local governments rely on the retail sales tax. In fiscal year 1974 federal excises accounted for only about 6 percent of federal budget receipts, while consumption taxes as a whole accounted for 15 percent of federal, state, and local revenues.

Consumption taxes are supported by those who believe that savings should not be taxed. They are not regarded as equitable, however, because the poor consume more of their income than do the rich, so that the burden of a general consumption tax lessens as incomes rise. Although excise taxes are occasionally progressive, on the whole they are regressive since they are usually levied on items consumed by a large proportion of the low and middle income population, whose consumption is not very sensitive to price.[13]

Sumptuary Taxes

The federal government derives most of its consumption tax revenue from excise taxes on commodities or services that are considered

12. Changes in revenue resulting from estate and gift tax reforms cannot be estimated by income classes because data on the distribution of wealth by income classes are scanty. But since wealth is heavily concentrated, reform of the estate and gift taxes would probably affect only the top 5 percent of the income distribution.

13. Excise taxes are usually levied on a unit basis; for example, 4 cents on a gallon of gasoline, $10.50 on a proof gallon of alcohol, 0.08 cents on a pack of cigarettes, and so forth. As a consequence, the tax as a percent of the price falls as prices increase. Whether this effect moderates the regressivity of excise taxes is unknown because there are no data on the changes in consumption of excise-taxed goods and services at various income levels during inflation.

socially and morally undesirable—for example, excises on the consumption of liquor and tobacco. The rationale for the sumptuary taxes is that use by consumers of the products on which the taxes are levied creates additional costs to society that are not borne by the producers and are not reflected in the prices they charge. For example, liquor consumption may impose costs in the form of loss of working time, accidents, and increased crime; and cigarette smoking has been shown to be associated with a wide range of illnesses. The excise tax raises the price of the commodity, thus discouraging consumption and at the same time imposing a charge on the people who are likely to create social problems.

Another type of excise tax is one whose proceeds are used to pay for particular services provided by government to consumers. The best example of such a tax is the gasoline tax, whose revenues have paid for the federal highway trust fund since its enactment in 1956. Special excise taxes have also been levied on airplane fuel and use of airports to pay for the federal airway system. The use of excise taxes in lieu of user charges is much more prevalent at the state and local government level, but they are used sparingly compared with their use in other countries.

Selective excise taxes are used heavily during wartime to discourage the consumption of items that are manufactured with strategic materials or are scarce for other reasons. During World War II most consumer durable goods (including automobiles and appliances) were taxed at rates up to 20 percent of the manufacturer's price. These taxes were phased out after the Korean War, and federal excise taxes are currently levied only on liquor and tobacco, telephone calls (scheduled to be phased out by 1982), and gasoline and other highway- and airway-related products and services. There is almost no support for greater use of selective excise taxes to raise revenues in peacetime.

Excise Taxes for Regulatory Purposes

Although selective excise taxes are hard to justify when used solely to raise revenue, they are frequently suggested as methods of regulating the use of particular goods or services or requiring private users to pay for the social costs of particular activities. When private businesses are allowed to pollute the rivers or the atmosphere, they impose heavy costs on society and yet are not required to pay for these costs. Consequently, production and consumption from such activities are artificially stimulated and too many resources are used. An excise tax, or other methods of charging for the cost, is needed to maintain economic efficiency.

In recent years economists have argued that pollution of water and air by private businesses and persons imposes heavy costs on society, which should not be borne by the general taxpayer. Instead of direct regulation, it should be possible to devise a system of effluent charges to discourage polluting activities and to raise revenues that might be used to defray government expenditures to clean up the rivers and the atmosphere.[14] It also seems appropriate to levy new, or more adequate, taxes and charges on individuals and businesses that benefit from the use of inland waterway transportation facilities, recreation facilities, and many other government-financed services.

The energy crisis has also directed attention to the possible use of special excise taxes as a method of reducing the demand for oil and other energy sources. Heavy taxes might be levied on gasoline, on large automobiles, and on energy consumption in general. Such taxes are usually much more efficient than direct regulation because they allow individuals and businesses to balance the costs of energy use against the benefits rather than having a government agency make the decisions for them. Special credits or refunds could be devised to alleviate the burden of such charges on low income families.

Despite the economic advantages, successive administrations have had little success in persuading the public and Congress to accept pollution and energy taxes. Such taxes are strongly resisted by the groups that would have to pay them, and it is difficult to find leaders who will take the political risks of fighting these groups.

A General Consumption Tax?

From time to time it is proposed that the federal government enact a general consumption tax as a replacement for some of the selective excise taxes or for other taxes in the tax system. In recent years most European countries and some developing countries have enacted a value-added tax, and suggestions that the United States follow suit are frequently made.

14. See Allen V. Kneese and Charles L. Schultze, *Pollution, Prices, and Public Policy* (Brookings Institution, 1975).

The value-added tax is essentially similar to a retail sales tax but is collected differently. A retail sales tax is levied on the price of goods and services purchased by individual consumers at the retail level. A value-added tax is one paid by all firms on the difference between their receipts from sales and their outlays for materials, supplies, and services. Provided the two taxes apply to the same commodities, the value-added tax collects the same amount as the retail sales tax, except that collections are made at all stages of production and distribution rather than at the retail level only.

Interest in a general consumption tax is strongest among those who believe that additional incentives are needed to promote saving. Income taxes are imposed on income that is saved as well as consumed, while consumption taxes are levied exclusively on consumption. The exclusion of saving from the tax base would provide more resources for investment and, at full employment, would tend to increase productivity and raise the rate of economic growth.

Retail sales and value-added taxes can with low rates produce large amounts of revenue because the taxable base is large. For example, at 1976 income levels the base would be about $775 billion if rents were exempted and about $550 billion if food consumed at home and medicine were also exempted. Thus a 2 percent retail sales or value-added tax could raise over $15 billion a year on the broad base and $11 billion a year on the narrow base.

The major objection to a general consumption tax is its regressivity. Many people believe that the revenue system of the United States is not progressive enough. The introduction of a general consumption tax would make matters worse unless it was accompanied by progressive tax reform.

In 1972 President Nixon requested the Advisory Commission on Intergovernmental Relations to examine the possibility of adopting a value-added tax and using the funds to replace a portion of the property taxes levied by local governments. To moderate the impact of the value-added tax on people with low and middle incomes, he suggested that a refundable credit might be allowed against the income tax for the estimated value-added tax paid by families with incomes below a certain level. However, the suggestion was dropped, partly because it is impractical to replace a tax used in varying degrees by local governments with a uniform federal tax and partly because of the opposition on equity grounds to value-added taxa-

Table 5-4. Comparison of Effective Tax Rates under a Value-Added Tax and an Individual Income Tax Surcharge of Equal Revenue Yield, 1972 Income Levels
Income classes in thousands of dollars; other numbers in percent

Income class[a]	Income tax surcharge[b]	Broad-base value-added tax with credit[c]	Narrow-base value-added tax[d]
0–3	0.1	0.1	1.8
3–5	0.2	0.6	1.5
5–10	0.6	0.8	1.5
10–15	1.0	1.1	1.4
15–20	1.3	1.7	1.4
20–25	1.4	1.9	1.3
25–50	1.7	1.7	1.2
50–100	2.6	1.1	0.7
100–500	3.5	0.8	0.5
500–1,000	3.9	0.4	0.2
1,000 and over	4.1	0.2	0.2
All classes[e]	1.3	1.3	1.3

Source: Based on the Brookings MERGE file of 30,000 family units for the year 1966, with incomes projected to 1972 level.

a. Income is equal to the sum of adjusted gross income, transfer payments, state and local government bond interest, and excluded realized long-term capital gains.

b. Surcharge of 11.8 percent on 1972 income tax liabilities.

c. Broad-base value-added tax at 3.25 percent with full credit up to $5,000 for a family of four; credit is phased out completely at $20,000.

d. Narrow-base value-added tax at 3.0 percent.

e. Includes negative income class not shown separately.

tion.[15] For example, the burden of a 3 percent value-added tax would fall from about 2 percent of income in the lowest income class to 0.2 percent in the highest classes (table 5-4, last column). Regressivity can be moderated or eliminated for the great majority of families by a credit or refund (second column), but it cannot be entirely eliminated at the top levels. By contrast, an income tax surcharge (first column) would be progressive throughout the income scale.

15. For a detailed analysis of the issues, see Advisory Commission on Intergovernmental Relations, *The Value-Added Tax and Alternative Sources of Federal Revenue* (ACIR, 1973).

CHAPTER SIX

Alternative Reform Packages

THE REFORMS discussed in the earlier chapters can be combined in various ways to achieve any number of objectives. In a few packages yielding the same revenue as the present tax laws, several different approaches that illustrate the potential of tax revision are given in this chapter. The objectives emphasized in these packages are, first, improvement of the progressivity of the federal tax system and, second, reduction of the marginal income tax rates applying to additions to individual income. Although seemingly contradictory, these objectives can be reconciled by broadening the income tax base to include items of income that are not now taxed or are given preferential rates and to eliminate unnecessary personal deductions.

The changes illustrated are confined to the three major taxes in the federal tax system: the individual income tax, the corporation income tax, and the payroll tax. Together these taxes accounted for 91 percent of federal tax revenues in fiscal year 1975 (see table 1-4). This is not to say that revision of the estate and gift taxes and the consumption taxes would not be desirable. As discussed in the previous chapter, the estate and gift taxes are urgently in need of reform, and greater use of excise taxation might be appropriate for environmental reasons. Nevertheless, such changes are omitted from the illustrations because revision of the estate and gift taxes is unlikely to raise significant amounts of revenue, and new excises would be enacted mainly to achieve objectives other than increased revenues or income redistribution.

Enactment of a general consumption tax is also excluded because such a tax would not be consistent with the progressivity objective. The regressive feature of a general consumption tax can be eliminated in the lower part of the income distribution by enacting a generous tax credit; but even with a credit, a general consumption tax would be regressive in the top brackets (table 5-4). Moreover, the retail sales tax is already a basic source of revenue for forty-five state governments and numerous local governments, and many would regard the enactment of a federal consumption tax as an unwarranted encroachment on this major revenue source.

The equal-yield constraint is particularly significant. The purpose of this chapter is *not* to show how federal revenues can be raised or lowered. Pure tax revision is neutral with respect to the yield objective. Income tax rates could be raised or lowered (in accordance with one of the formulas suggested in chapter 2) once the structure of the tax system had been perfected and was regarded by most people as fair. If this happened, temporary changes in the tax rate—either upward or downward—to promote economic stability could be enacted without the long delays experienced in recent years.

Elements of Reform

The elements of tax reform brought together here range from fairly modest changes that would leave the present tax system basically the same to drastic revisions that would fundamentally alter the taxation of labor and capital income.

The Individual Income Tax

The major problems in the individual income tax are how to treat capital gains, interest on state and local government bonds, personal deductions, and two-earner married couples.

CAPITAL GAINS. Taxation of unrealized capital gains transferred by gift or at death is regarded by many as a prerequisite of rational taxation of capital gains. Treating such gains as if they were constructively realized would encourage taxpayers to turn over their assets when alternative investment opportunities appeared rather than delaying to avoid the capital gains tax. Constructive realization could be adopted without any changes in the taxation of realized capital gains, or all capital gains could be taxed as ordinary income at greatly reduced tax rates (particularly in the top brackets where capital gains are heavily concentrated). An intermediate possibility would be to retain the present 50 percent exclusion for long-term capital gains but to lengthen the holding period separating short- from long-term gains from six months to a year and eliminate the 25 percent maximum tax on the first $50,000 of long-term gains. If the tax rates on capital gains and ordinary incomes are not equalized, consideration might be given to improving the base for the tax on preference income (the minimum tax) and raising the tax rate to half the ordinary rate. Corresponding changes would apply to the capital gains and preference income of corporations.

STATE-LOCAL BOND INTEREST. Immediate taxation of interest on state and local bonds already issued would drive down the price of these bonds and subject the owners to huge losses. It is widely agreed, therefore, that any changes in the income tax status of such bonds should be made only for future issues. The plan that seems to be most appealing to both tax reformers and state and local officials would give the states and local governments the option to issue taxable securities, the interest on which would be heavily subsidized by the federal government. Since the plan would apply only prospectively, the revenue effect would be relatively small in the early years. For this reason, the revenue estimates presented in this chapter do not make allowance for any revision in the treatment of state-local bond interest.

PERSONAL DEDUCTIONS. Although the personal deductions are a major drain on the individual income tax base, most of them would be difficult to dislodge. It might be desirable, however, to prune the clearly unnecessary or inequitable deductions and to reduce the tax rates correspondingly. A modest program might include eliminating the deduction for state gasoline taxes and property taxes, increasing the floor for medical expense deductions from 3 to 5 percent, treating health insurance premiums like other medical expenses, and limiting the deduction for interest payments on loans to the amount of property and business income reported by the taxpayer plus $2,000. These changes would reduce the tax advantages of homeowners (without disturbing the deduction of interest paid on mortgages of most owner-occupied homes), remove the federal tax subsidy given to consumers of gasoline, limit the deduction for medical expenses to those that are clearly unusual, and prevent tax avoidance through borrowing. If these changes were made, it would be possible to remove the percentage standard deduction and to rely entirely on the minimum standard deduction (or low-income allowance). The itemized deductions that would remain unchanged would include the deductions for state and local income and sales taxes, charitable contributions, outlays for child care, alimony, and business-related expenses.

TWO-EARNER MARRIED COUPLES. With the increasing participation of women in the labor force, the discrimination that results from omitting from the tax base the value of services of spouses who remain at home has become serious. Not only are two-earner couples thereby at a disadvantage, but the participation of the second earner is greatly discouraged by the high tax rates imposed on his or her earnings. One remedy is to provide a special tax credit for two-earner married couples, say, 10 percent of the earnings of the spouse with the lower earnings up to $1,000. At the same time, the complicated set of rates now required because of the income splitting provision could be replaced by one set of rates applying to all taxpayers. For illustrative purposes, the new rate schedule is taken to be the one that applied before the income splitting amendment was passed—that is, the rates now used by married couples filing separate returns. An alternative is to permit single persons to use the same rate schedule as married couples filing joint returns. The resulting distribution of tax burdens would not be very different because the tax rates would be adjusted to yield the same amount of revenue. Under either approach, married persons filing separate returns would be required to use a schedule with the same tax rates as those applying to other taxpayers but with brackets that were half as wide as the regular brackets.

The Payroll Tax

The payroll tax places a heavy burden on low-income earners. Two approaches to remedy this defect are considered here. First, employees and the self-employed could be allowed to deduct the same per capita exemptions and low-income allowance as are provided under the individual income tax. To limit the tax reduction to those at the bottom of the income scale, the deduction could be phased out gradually for incomes above the minimum taxable levels. Under this alternative, no change would be made in the payroll tax paid by employers. Second, the payroll tax could be converted to a progressive tax on earnings by removing the taxable earnings ceiling and allowing exemptions and the low-income allowance without a phase-out. This would be applicable to the taxes paid by employers as well as to those paid by employees and the self-employed. Revenues from the payroll tax could be preserved by raising the rate on the earnings subject to tax.

The Corporation Income Tax

Revision of the corporation income tax base might begin with the removal of the preferential treatment now accorded to specific types of business or property income. Chief among these are the percentage depletion allowances for oil, gas, and other minerals, the preferential rate on long-term capital gains, and the deferral of tax on foreign income and on half the income of domestic international sales corporations (DISCs).[1] Beyond such changes, the major issue is whether the corporation and individual income taxes should be integrated in whole or in part. To show the implications of integration, calculations will be shown for a plan that would impute corporate earnings to persons and tax them at individual income tax rates.[2] The rates are adjusted to offset the revenue loss, but top bracket rates are limited to a maximum of close to 50 percent to avoid impairment of saving and investment incentives.

Reform Options

The tax liabilities for 1976 under the individual and corporation income taxes and the payroll tax are estimated to aggregate $260 billion, or 24 percent of the income of all those filing tax returns.[3]

1. Except for the deferral features, the other provisions are also applicable to the individual income tax. Revision of the corporation income tax base would presumably be accompanied by similar changes in the individual income tax base.

2. The corporation tax could be retained as a withholding tax, which would be credited to taxpayers on their individual income tax returns. The imputation of corporate earnings to individuals could be left to the corporations along the lines recommended by the Canadian Royal Commission on Taxation (see pages 101–02).

3. The income concept used in these calculations approximates a comprehensive definition of income, including undistributed corporate profits before taxes but excluding transfer payments. The calculations were made by adding to adjusted gross income (as defined by the tax code) the share of corporate retained earnings and the corporate tax allocable to individuals (distributed on the basis of dividends received), half of the capital gains transferred at gift or death, the excess of percentage

Table 6-1. Effective Federal Rates of Individual and Corporation Income and Payroll Taxes under Present Law and under Four Reform Options, by Comprehensive Income Class, 1976

Income classes in thousands of dollars; other numbers in percent

Comprehensive income class[a]	Present law	Option A	Option B	Option C	Option D
0–5	11.3	8.2	3.8	3.6	3.1
5–10	18.2	16.4	12.3	12.7	11.6
10–15	21.4	20.6	16.7	17.3	16.1
15–20	22.9	22.9	20.6	21.6	20.2
20–25	23.6	23.6	24.0	25.0	23.5
25–50	25.2	25.3	30.7	31.2	30.0
50–100	31.9	32.8	41.0	39.1	41.8
100–200	36.0	39.4	45.7	42.7	50.4
200–500	39.3	44.8	48.7	44.5	55.7
500–1,000	42.1	49.4	51.2	45.4	58.6
1,000 and over	41.9	52.1	51.9	44.5	58.3
All classes[b]	24.0	24.0	24.0	24.0	24.0

Source: Brookings 1970 tax file, projected to 1976. The options are explained in the text.

a. Includes adjusted gross income, the share of corporate retained earnings and the corporate tax allocated to individuals, half of total estimated capital gains transferred by gift or death, excess of percentage depletion over cost depletion, and interest on state and local government bonds.

b. Includes negative incomes not shown separately.

Under the tax laws in effect for calendar year 1975 the aggregate of these taxes would amount to an estimated 11.3 percent of income below $5,000, rise to 25.2 percent of incomes between $25,000 and $50,000, and reach 41.9 percent of incomes of $1,000,000 and over (see table 6-1). When the tax returns are divided according to population deciles,[4] the effective tax rate begins at 10.6 percent in the first decile, rises to 22.0 percent in the fifth decile, and to 32.5 percent in the top decile (see table 6-2).

Option A: Modest Reform

The effective rate curve can be tilted in a progressive direction by a relatively modest revision of the payroll tax and increases in the tax

depletion over cost depletion, and interest on state and local government bonds. Only half of the realized capital gains and of the gains considered to be constructively realized at transfer by gift or death are included in income because, since retained corporate profits account for approximately half of all capital gains, full taxation of corporate earnings would eliminate half of the capital gains generated under the present system.

4. The deciles are based on the distribution of all single persons and families by size of income.

Table 6-2. Effective Federal Rates of Individual and Corporation Income and Payroll Taxes under Present Law and under Four Reform Options, by Population Decile, 1976

Percent

Population decile[a]		Present law	Option A	Option B	Option C	Option D
First	($3,400)	10.6	6.3	1.5	1.1	0.8
Second	($6,350)	13.6	11.6	7.7	7.8	6.9
Third	($9,300)	18.5	16.7	12.4	12.8	11.7
Fourth	($12,300)	20.6	19.3	15.4	15.9	14.7
Fifth	($15,150)	22.0	21.5	17.7	18.4	17.1
Sixth	($18,000)	22.7	22.7	20.0	21.0	19.6
Seventh	($21,850)	23.4	23.4	22.3	23.4	21.9
Eighth	($25,650)	23.9	23.9	25.1	26.0	24.4
Ninth	($32,950)	24.5	24.6	28.8	29.4	27.9
Tenth		32.5	34.9	41.3	39.2	43.6
All deciles[b]		24.0	24.0	24.0	24.0	24.0

Source: Brookings 1970 tax file, projected to 1976.

a. Population deciles are in order of comprehensive income ranked from low to high. For definition of comprehensive income, see table 6-1, note a. Figures in parentheses are the top income limits of the deciles, which are based on the distribution of all single persons and families by size of income. The 1976 limits were obtained by extrapolation from 1966 on the basis of the increase in national income per capita. Data for 1966 are from Joseph A. Pechman and Benjamin A. Okner, *Who Bears the Tax Burden?* (Brookings Institution, 1974).

b. Includes negative incomes not shown separately.

on preference income under the individual income tax (see table 6-3).

The change in the payroll tax would relieve low-income earners from paying the employee's share of the tax by introducing an exemption of $900 per capita and a low-income allowance of $2,000. This means that a wage earner with a family of four would not be subject to payroll tax until his earnings reached $5,600. To confine the tax reduction to the lowest end of the income scale, the exemption and low-income allowance would be phased out by $1 for every $2 of earnings above the minimum taxable level. The payroll tax paid by the employer would remain unchanged, and the earned-income credit enacted in 1975 would be repealed. To preserve the financial status of the social security system, the loss in revenue would be reimbursed to the trust funds out of general revenues.

The income tax revisions would eliminate the percentage depletion allowance on oil, gas, and other minerals, modify the tax on capital gains, and raise the tax on preference income. The major change in the capital gains tax would be the inclusion of gains transferred by

Table 6-3. Summary of Structural Revisions under Four Reform Options

Item	Option A	Option B	Option C	Option D
Capital gains				
Increase holding period from six months to one year	×	a	a	a
Eliminate alternative tax	×	a	a	a
Tax capital gains as ordinary income	...	×	×	×
Constructive realization of capital gains	×	×	×	×
Tax on preference income				
Reduce $30,000 exemption to $5,000	×	a	a	a
Eliminate deduction for taxes	×	a	a	a
Raise tax rates to one-half the ordinary rates (present base)	×	a	a	a
Personal deductions				
Eliminate state gasoline tax deduction	...	×	×	×
Eliminate separate health insurance premium deduction	...	×	×	×
Raise medical expense floor from 3 to 5 percent	...	×	×	×
Eliminate property tax deduction	...	×	×	×
Limit interest deduction to property and business income plus $2,000	...	×	×	×
Repeal percentage standard deduction and raise low-income allowance to $3,000	...	×	×	×
Treatment of married couples and single people				
Remove rate advantages of income splitting	...	×	×	×
Provide 10 percent tax credit (up to $1,000) for spouse with lower earnings	...	×	×	×
Other provisions				
Eliminate percentage depletion	×	×	×	×
Eliminate deferral through DISCs	...	×	×	×
Eliminate deferral of income of foreign-controlled corporations	...	×	×	×
Eliminate dividend exclusion	...	×	×	×
Eliminate maximum tax on earned income	...	×	×	×
Repeal tax on preference income	...	×	×	×
Payroll tax				
Introduce $900 per capita exemption and $2,000 low-income allowance, with phase-out of $1 for every $2 of earnings (employee and self-employed only)	×	...	...	...
Introduce $900 per capita exemption and $2,000 low-income allowance; eliminate ceiling on maximum taxable earnings; raise tax rate by 1.7 percentage points (employee, employer, and self-employed)	...	×	×	×
Integration				
Tax all corporate earnings to shareholders at individual income tax rates[b]	...	...	×	×

a. Revision not relevant because capital gains would be taxed in full.
b. Tax-exempt organizations are assumed not taxed on their allocated share of corporate earnings.

gift or death in the tax base. In addition, the holding period separating short- from long-term gains would be lengthened from six months to a year, and the alternative tax of 25 percent on the first $50,000 of capital gains would be eliminated. The base of the tax on preference income would be broadened by reducing the present $30,000 exemption to $5,000 and by eliminating the deduction for taxes; and the rates of the tax would be increased from a flat 10 percent to half the ordinary rates (that is, from a minimum of 7 percent to a maximum of 35 percent). In effect, these revisions would raise the maximum marginal tax rate on long-term capital gains from 36.5 percent under present law to 52.5 percent.[5]

The effect of this package would be to finance payroll tax reductions for low-income earners by revisions that would affect mainly the taxes paid by high-income taxpayers and corporations. As a result, average income and payroll tax burdens would be reduced in the income classes below $15,000, which account for about 50 percent of all family units, and raised for incomes above $25,000, or the top 20 percent of the family units.[6] The tax reductions are substantial at the bottom of the income scale—over 25 percent below $5,000—while the tax increases are relatively moderate for all but the highest incomes—only about 3 percent for incomes between $50,000 and $100,000 and 24 percent for $1,000,000 and over. Average effective rates would range from 8.2 percent on income below $5,000 to 52.1 percent on income of $1,000,000 and above; under present law the range is 11.3 to 41.9 percent.

Option B: Ambitious Reform

Although Option A increases the progressivity of the federal tax structure, it does little to reduce the erosion of the two income taxes and to improve horizontal equity. Moreover, because its revisions

5. Under present law, the maximum rate is one-half of the top bracket rate (35 percent) plus 10 percent of the difference between the half of capital gains excluded from the tax base and the tax paid on the half that is included (1.5 percent), making a total of 36.5 percent. (If the maximum tax on earned income is used by the taxpayer, the maximum rate on capital gains is even higher.) Under the revision, the maximum rate would be one-half of the top bracket rate (35 percent) plus the tax on the half of the gains excluded from the tax base at half the ordinary rate (17.5 percent), which is a total of 52.5 percent.

6. In this and subsequent calculations, corporate tax changes are distributed in accordance with the dividends reported on tax returns. This assumes that changes in the corporate tax either benefit or are borne by stockholders.

are limited, it is necessary to keep tax rates on ordinary income at present levels. Option B would remove the major eroding features of the income tax, convert the payroll tax to a progressive tax on earnings, retain the corporation income tax, and reduce the individual income tax rates substantially. It should be noted that Option B, by taxing capital gains in full and retaining a separate corporation tax, would increase the excess burdens—and reduce the excess benefits— on income from corporate sources shown in table 4-2.

The major income tax changes would be to treat capital gains as ordinary income, including gains transferred by gift or death; eliminate percentage depletion, deferral of tax through the DISC arrangements, and deferral of income of foreign-controlled corporations; remove the dividend exclusion, the maximum tax on earned income, and the tax on preference income; greatly reduce the itemized personal deductions;[7] and raise the standard deduction to a flat $3,000. In addition the rate advantages of income splitting would be removed, and married couples with two earners would be given a tax credit of 10 percent of the earnings of the spouse with the lower earnings up to a maximum of $1,000.

The payroll tax on both employees and employers would be revised to apply only to earnings above a minimum of $900 per capita plus a standard deduction of $2,000, without a maximum taxable earnings limit. To offset the revenue loss, the tax rate would be raised by 1.7 percentage points.

Since at present rates the income tax reforms under Option B would increase tax liabilities by about $60 billion a year, the tax rates could be reduced very substantially. To raise the revenues now raised by the individual income tax, the tax rates could be lowered from the present range of 14 to 70 percent to a range of 10 to 50 percent (see table 6-4).

The major effect of Option B would be to reduce income and payroll tax burdens in the lower 70 percent of the income distribution and raise those on incomes in the top 30 percent (table 6-2). A major share of this increase in progressivity is accounted for by the conver-

7. The specific changes are as follows: eliminate the deductions for state gasoline taxes and property taxes; treat health insurance premiums like other medical expenses and raise the floor for the medical expense deduction from 3 to 5 percent of income; and limit the deduction for interest payments to income from property and business plus $2,000.

Table 6-4. Marginal Individual Income Tax Rate Schedules under Present Law
and under Four Reform Options, by Taxable Income Class
Income classes in thousands of dollars; other figures in percent

Taxable income class	Present law and Option A[a]	Taxable income class	Option B[b]	Option C[b]	Oprion D[b]
Under 1	14	Under 0.5	10	12	8
1–2	15	0.5–1	11	13	10
2–3	16	1–1.5	12	14	12
3–4	17	1.5–2	13	16	14
4–8	19	2–4	15	18	16
8–12	22	4–6	17	20	18
12–16	25	6–8	19	22	20
16–20	28	8–10	21	24	22
20–24	32	10–12	23	26	24
24–28	36	12–14	25	28	26
28–32	39	14–16	27	30	28
32–36	42	16–18	30	33	30
36–40	45	18–20	33	36	34
40–44	48	20–22	36	39	38
44–52	50	22–26	39	42	42
52–64	53	26–32	41	44	46
64–76	55	32–38	42	45	50
76–88	58	38–44	43	46	53
88–100	60	44–50	44	47	56
100–120	62	50–60	45	48	59
120–140	64	60–70	46	49	62
140–160	66	70–80	47	50	64
160–180	68	80–90	48	51	66
180–200	69	90–100	49	52	68
200 and over	70	100 and over	50	53	70

a. Rate schedule for married couples filing joint returns. Couples filing separate returns use the same rates but with brackets half as wide as those shown above. Single persons and heads of households use rate schedules that fall between the schedules for separate and joint returns of married couples.

b. Rate schedule used by all taxpayers regardless of marital status.

sion of the payroll tax to a progressive tax on earnings. For persons with income below $5,000, the average effective rate of tax under Option B would be only 3.8 percent as against 8.2 percent under Option A and 11.3 percent under present law. For incomes between $50,000 and $100,000, the effective rate would be 41.0 percent under Option B, 32.8 percent under Option A, and 31.9 percent under present law. Because the top-bracket rate is limited to 50 percent, progressivity tapers off as incomes rise above $1,000,000. For income of $1,000,000 or more, the effective rates are slightly lower under Option B than under Option A, but higher than under present law—51.9 percent under Option B,[8] 52.1 percent under Option A, and 41.9 percent under present law (table 6-1).

Another important effect of the revisions in Option B is the reduction of the wide disparities in tax liabilities among people with the same income. Option B would lower the tax burdens of single people relative to those of married couples, of two-earner married couples relative to one-earner couples, of renters relative to homeowners, of recipients of ordinary income relative to recipients of capital gains, and of those who use the standard deduction relative to those who itemize deductions.

Option B would also greatly simplify the tax laws for the majority of taxpayers. The major improvement would be the elimination of any distinction between capital gains and other income. This would get rid of large sections of the Internal Revenue Code that are now needed to distinguish capital gains from other income. In addition, taxpayers would not have to keep track of so many itemized deductions, and a single set of tax rates would be substituted for the four sets of rates now required because of income splitting and the provisions associated with it.

Options C and D: Ambitious Reform with Integration

The final two options would combine integration of the individual and corporation income taxes with the reforms under Option B. Integration is achieved in these options by taxing all corporate earnings to shareholders at individual income tax rates.[9] Two alternatives are presented for the integration calculations to show the effect of different schedules of tax rates. In Option C, an attempt was made to hold the top marginal tax rate as close to 50 percent as possible and still produce the same revenue as the combined total of the individual and corporation income taxes under present law. In Option D, the top bracket rate was held at the present 70 percent and all other tax rates were adjusted downward to yield the same revenue. Option C rates,

8. The average effective rate exceeds 50 percent under Option B even though the top-bracket individual income tax rate is 50 percent, because the separate corporation income tax is retained in this option.

9. The tax burdens (though not the amount of earnings that corporations would be able to retain) do not depend on whether the corporation income tax is preserved. It is likely that the government would set the corporation tax at or near the top-bracket individual income tax rate as a withholding device to prevent wholesale delinquency in tax payments by shareholders.

which begin at 12 percent and reach 53 percent in the top bracket, are 2 percentage points higher than Option B rates in the taxable income brackets below $1,500 and 3 percentage points higher at $1,500 and over. This method of adjusting the tax rates was chosen to make the necessary tax rate increases in a progressive manner while keeping the top-bracket rate increase to a minimum. Option D rates range from 8 percent at the bottom to 70 percent at the top, while under present law the range is 14 to 70 percent.[10]

The most significant effect of integration at Option C tax rates would be to reduce income and payroll tax burdens from those borne under Option B in the lowest and highest deciles and to raise them in the eight intermediate deciles (table 6-2). For incomes below $5,000, the average effective rate is 3.6 percent under Option C and 3.8 percent under Option B. Between $5,000 and $50,000, the tax burdens are slightly larger under Option C than under Option B; at $50,000 and above, tax burdens are reduced and by larger proportions as incomes increase. For example, for incomes between $100,000 and $200,000, the average effective rates would be 42.7 percent under Option C and 45.7 percent under Option B. For incomes of $1,000,000 or more, the average effective rates would be 44.5 percent under Option C and 51.9 percent under Option B. In the top bracket, the effect of the low tax rate would be so large that effective rates under Option C would be only 6 percent higher than the effective rates under present law despite the major overhaul of the individual income tax base (table 6-1).

Option D would increase effective tax rates in the top decile substantially and lower them for the rest of the distribution. In the top decile, the average effective rates would be 43.6 percent under Option D and 39.2 percent under Option C (table 6-2). Within the decile, the tax increases become relatively larger as incomes rise. For incomes between $100,000 and $200,000, the average effective rate would be 50.4 percent under Option D and 42.7 percent under Option C. At $1,000,000 and above, the effective rates are 58.3 percent

10. For Options C and D, it is assumed that the revenue lost from integration is fully recovered from individual income taxpayers and that tax-exempt organizations remain tax exempt. If a special excise tax of $12.5 billion were levied on the corporate income of tax-exempt organizations to recover the revenue now collected from such income under the corporation tax, the Option C and D tax rates could be reduced by about 1 percentage point across the board.

and 44.5 percent under Options D and C respectively. Thus if the tax rates in the top brackets were kept close to those under present law, integration would increase progressivity. If the top-bracket rates were reduced, the progressivity of the income taxes would be reduced and might even be impaired unless structural revisions (similar to those included in Option B) were made at the same time.

Conclusions

Although on balance the federal tax system is progressive, tax burdens in the lowest income classes are heavy and the rate of progression throughout the income scale is relatively moderate. Moreover, the income taxes do not apply uniformly to all incomes, and this leads to wide differences in the tax treatment of people who receive the same total income from different sources. Although tax rates reach a maximum of 70 percent, the average effective rate is substantially less than 50 percent of the total income in the highest income classes.

The heavy tax burden at the low end of the income scale is due almost entirely to the payroll tax. The personal exemptions and minimum standard deduction under the individual income tax are periodically adjusted to exclude from the income tax rolls those whose incomes are below the poverty levels as defined by the federal government. By contrast, the payroll tax is levied at a uniform rate from the first dollar of earnings to a maximum of $14,100 for 1975 and $15,300 for 1976. A 10 percent earned-income credit on earnings up to $4,000 (with a phase-out between $4,000 and $8,000) is provided under the income tax for earners with children. Thus the payroll tax for earners without children is a proportional tax on earnings below the maximum taxable limit and is regressive beyond that point.

The heavy burden the payroll tax places on low incomes can be lifted by introducing the individual income tax exemptions and minimum standard deduction into the calculations of payroll tax liabilities. This would permit the repeal of the earned-income credit. The regressivity of the payroll tax can be remedied by eliminating the maximum taxable earnings limit.[11] Revenues from the payroll tax

11. Social security benefits are now based on percentages of earnings up to the maximum taxable limit under the payroll tax. If the limit were lifted completely, a separate decision would have to be made regarding the benefit calculations. Presumably, the maximum earnings on which the benefits are based would be raised but not completely removed. See note 4, page 108 above.

could be maintained at the present level, if desired, by increasing the payroll tax rate. At 1976 earnings levels, the required rate increase would be 1.7 percentage points for both employees and employers.

Many features of the income taxes that treat different incomes differently should be reconsidered. Some have been in the tax laws since their inception without being subject to congressional scrutiny; others are considered essential to encourage particular types of business activities or to promote saving and investment; still others are justified on the ground that the regular income tax rates are too high. If capital gains and all other income sources were taxed at the same rates and unnecessary personal deductions were eliminated, it would be possible to bring the tax rates down to a maximum of 50 percent and still increase the progressivity of the individual income tax moderately. Tax reform along these lines would improve horizontal as well as vertical equity, increase incentives to earn additional income through greater work effort and risk-taking, promote a better allocation of economic resources, and simplify tax administration and compliance.

The present system of taxing corporate income and then taxing dividends in full under the individual income tax places a heavier burden on income generated in the corporate sector than on other income. The extra burden of the corporation tax has also been attacked as a regressive feature of the tax system, since it is much larger for low-income stockholders than for those in the higher income classes. On the other hand, the taxation of corporate income is staunchly defended by its proponents as a major element of progressivity in the tax system. These contradictory judgments reflect different opinions about what tax rates might be if the two taxes were integrated. The progressivity of the present system would be increased if the top-bracket tax rates under an integrated tax were maintained at or close to present levels. On the other hand, substantial reduction of the top-bracket rates would lessen the progressivity of the income taxes. If integration were combined with other base-broadening revisions and the top tax rate were lowered to about 50 percent, income tax burdens would be reduced in the lowest income classes, increased slightly in the highest income classes, and increased substantially for those in between.

Selected Bibliography

Blechman, Barry M., Edward M. Gramlich, and Robert W. Hartman. *Setting National Priorities: The 1976 Budget.* Washington: Brookings Institution, 1975.

Break, George F. "The Incidence and Economic Effects of Taxation," in Alan S. Blinder and others, *The Economics of Public Finance.* Brookings Institution, 1974.

Brittain, John A. *The Payroll Tax for Social Security.* Brookings Institution, 1972.

David, Martin. *Alternative Approaches to Capital Gains Taxation.* Brookings Institution, 1968.

Due, John F. *Sales Taxation.* Urbana: University of Illinois Press, 1957.

Fromm, Gary, ed. *Tax Incentives and Capital Spending.* Brookings Institution, 1971.

Goode, Richard. *The Corporation Income Tax.* New York: Wiley, 1951.
———. *The Individual Income Tax.* Rev. ed. Brookings Institution, 1975.

Groves, Harold M. *Federal Tax Treatment of the Family.* Brookings Institution, 1963.

Kahn, C. Harry. *Personal Deductions in the Federal Income Tax.* Princeton: Princeton University Press for the National Bureau of Economic Research, 1960.

McLure, Charles E., Jr. "Integration of the Personal and Corporate Income Taxes: The Missing Element in Recent Tax Reform Proposals," *Harvard Law Review,* vol. 88 (January 1975).

Musgrave, Peggy B. *United States Taxation of Foreign Investment Income: Issues and Arguments.* Cambridge: Harvard University Law School, 1969.

Musgrave, Richard A., ed. *Broad-Based Taxes: New Options and Sources.* Baltimore: Johns Hopkins University Press, 1973.

———, and Peggy B. Musgrave. *Public Finance in Theory and Practice.* New York: McGraw-Hill, 1973.

Pechman, Joseph A. *Federal Tax Policy.* Rev. ed. Brookings Institution, 1971.

———, and Benjamin A. Okner. *Who Bears the Tax Burden?* Brookings Institution, 1974.

Seltzer, Lawrence H. *The Nature and Tax Treatment of Capital Gains and Losses.* New York: National Bureau of Economic Research, 1951.

Shoup, Carl S. *Federal Estate and Gift Taxes.* Brookings Institution, 1966.

Simons, Henry C. *Federal Tax Reform.* Chicago: University of Chicago Press, 1950.

———. *Personal Income Taxation.* University of Chicago Press, 1938.

Smith, Dan Throop. *Federal Tax Reform: The Issues and a Program.* New York: McGraw-Hill, 1961.

Stern, Philip M. *The Rape of the Taxpayer.* New York: Random House, 1973.

Surrey, Stanley S. *Pathways to Tax Reform: The Concept of Tax Expenditures.* Cambridge: Harvard University Press, 1973.

The Role of Direct and Indirect Taxes in the Federal Revenue System. Princeton University Press, 1964.

U.S. Congress. House. Committee on Ways and Means. *General Tax Reform.* Panel Discussions. 11 parts. Washington: Government Printing Office, 1973.

———. *Tax Revision Compendium.* Papers on Broadening the Tax Base. 3 vols. Government Printing Office, 1959.

U.S. Congress. Joint Publication, House Committee on Ways and Means and Senate Committee on Finance. *Tax Reform Studies and Proposals, U.S. Treasury Department.* 4 parts. Government Printing Office, 1969.

Index

139